The American Frontier

Table of Contents

—The American Frontier: an Introduction—

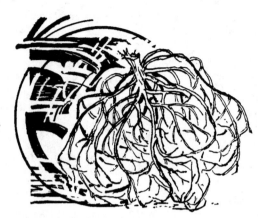

It is a story filled with adventure, risk, courage, tragedy, and dreams. It is a saga of movement and endurance; of seeking a new place and a better life, a search for what lies beyond the next mountain, the next river, the next forest, and the next rolling prairie. Those who were a part of its unfolding drama and myth—Daniel Boone, Lewis and Clark, Zebulon Pike, Davy Crockett, Kit Carson, Sam Houston, Buffalo Bill—continue to inspire the imaginations of many readers and spark our curiosity with scenes of trailblazing, fur trapping, buffalo hunting, and empire building.

It is the story of the American frontier. A constant thread throughout the history of the developing United States, the era of the American frontier reveals the stories of those who led the way west; those who helped to tame and settle the lands which today comprise a nation of over 280 million people with its mix of races, nationalities, and ethnic diversity.

So much of this period of American history is clouded over with legends, tall tales, and well-intended mythology, it is sometimes difficult to separate fact from fiction. Everyone knows that Daniel Boone, the great Kentucky trailblazer, wore a coonskin cap; that Davy Crockett went to his death at the Alamo swinging his empty Kentucky rifle against Mexican soldiers; that Indians were cruel and savage people who stood in the way of American progress; that Lewis and Clark were the first white men to reach the Great Plains and the Rocky Mountains; and that wagon trains on the Oregon Trail regularly faced the threat of Indian attack and so circled their wagons, as warriors on horseback rode endlessly around the circular caravan, their war whoops echoing across the Plains.

In fact, all those "facts" are false. Daniel Boone did not like wearing coonskin caps. Instead, he wore felt hats. Davy Crockett probably surrendered at the Alamo and was executed after the battle was over. Native Americans were not typically cruel and savage, but rather were themselves victims of deceit at the hands of Anglo-Americans and the federal government. Lewis and Clark, in fact, encountered other white men on their expedition, including a fur trader named Charbonneau, who was "married" to Sacajawea, the famous Indian guide. And Indian attack against wagon trains rarely happened at all.

How, then, do we come to have such enduring images of the American frontier which are simply untrue or misleading? A portion of the answer lies in how the westward movement has been portrayed on television and in motion pictures, as well as in American literature.

Throughout nearly all of the 20th century, motion pictures have portrayed the frontier as a place filled with brave pioneers, treacherous Indians, intrepid mountain men, and cowboys ready to fight for the underdog. In fact, the first motion picture with a plot was a western, *The Great Train Robbery*, filmed in 1903.

Television programs, beginning in the 1950s, and even more recently, regularly included "westerns" in their evening lineups—from *Gunsmoke* to *Bonanza*; *The Young Riders* to *Dr. Quinn, Medicine Woman*. Such programs typically bypassed the true reality of western life: hard work, crude living conditions, and little glamour.

Popular fiction has also often distorted the true nature of the American frontier, the West of the imagination, with images of gunfighters, barroom brawls, and swaggering cowboys ready to draw down at the flick of a well-trained wrist.

The purpose of this book is to draw an accurate and realistic picture of what life was like on the frontier. The true story, as you will see, can be as exciting as the myth.

The Moveable Frontier

Before taking up the history of the American West or the frontier movement in American history, it is important to have a clear understanding of at least two historical terms, both of which have already been used in this introductory sentence: the West and the frontier.

What exactly is meant by each of these two terms? Do they refer to the same thing? And if they do, what is that "thing"? Is the West a place or a time period? Where, specifically, is the frontier? Answers for these questions are not as easy as they seem.

To begin, let's attempt to nail down a definition for the term, frontier. After all, it's part of the title of this book. The term frontier generally refers to a marginal reality lying between two places. In some respects, those 'two places' can be identified as the known and the unknown. When an Englishman sailed in 1607 from his home in England (the known) to the site later called Jamestown in colonial Virginia, he landed in an America he had never seen before (the unknown). That place where he settled (Fort James, or later Jamestown) was a marginal reality called the frontier.

We can identify the term frontier, as it related to American history, then, as the place lying between civilization (the known) and the wilderness (the unknown). Obviously, that Jamestown settler of 1607 came to live in the wilderness, an untamed land of virgin forests, unpolluted rivers, and unspoiled meadows. But, simply by his being there, having left another place behind, and bringing with him Old World skills, ways of thinking, values, traditions, technologies, and social institutions, the wilderness he occupied did not remain wild.

In time, the Jamestown colonist and thousands like him, felled the trees, built houses and a fort, established churches, organized themselves socially, elected representatives to an assembly, farmed the meadows, and tamed their world. Once these changes were introduced (and many others besides), the marginal existence of life in Jamestown ended and Old World civilization, as well as New World influences, came together to create a new civilization in America. As that process progressed, the frontier, in that place, ceased to exist.

The frontier experience in our example at Jamestown, then, lasted from 1607 through a generation or so, then ended. Once civilization alters the wilderness, that region can no longer be called wilderness. Those years of transition are frontier years. So, the "frontier" in American history was a place always in transition.

This means that the frontier was always moving, as well. As people moved west, they established new settlements, each attached to a new wilderness place, and the process of taming the frontier and establishing the elements of civilization began all over again.

Defining "the West" is equally tricky. In the first place, "west" refers to a geographical location or direction. But when used in connection with "the frontier," it is not only a direction, it is a region. And, just as with the frontier, where "the West" was depended on where people were at the time. For a resident of 17th-century Jamestown, "the West" was the Appalachian Mountains and the Piedmont region. For the pioneer of 1750, "the West" was Kentucky, Ohio, and Tennessee. For those who migrated along the Oregon Trail a century later, "the West" might be California or Oregon.

The West, then, as a place, has constantly changed throughout American history. As people and time moved, so did the places known as the West and the frontier. Both terms refer to a place, perhaps of the imagination, which was always evolving into somewhere else.

Review and Write

In defining "the frontier," it is necessary to distinguish it from another term, "the West." While they might overlap, the two terms have different definitions. Explain the differences between "the West" and "the frontier."

Two Great Frontiers

An examination of the American Frontier is actually a study of at least two frontier periods in U.S. history. The first spanned the decades from approximately 1750 and 1850. This was the era of the Trans-Appalachian frontier. This frontier era included the expansion of Anglo- Americans west to the Appalachian Mountains and beyond, to the lands lying just west of the Mississippi River.

During this period, two great migrations of people moved across the frontier. The first migration pushed its way west to the Mississippi Valley, while, later, the second included settlers from the East and Midwest who moved across to the Great Plains in huge caravans of wagons bound for Oregon or California.

The second era was a shorter period of time, but one filled with kinetic movement and ultimate settlement of people across the Great Plains, west of the Mississippi River, throughout the Rocky Mountain region and the Pacific Coast. This period, from 1850 to 1890, marks the establishment of the Western Frontier, or the Trans-Mississippi West. It was a world of the cowboys, the open range, stage-coaches and the transcontinental railroad, Homesteaders, and rollicking mining towns.

Before taking up the subject of the Trans-Appalachian Frontier, a bit of background is needed. From the early 1600s, Europeans had landed by the boatload along the Atlantic seaboard, establishing colonial outposts, trading centers, plantations, and hopeful communities of immigrant-settlers, all eager to make a new place for themselves in America. While many of those who settled in the colonies stretching from New Hampshire and Massachusetts to the southern settlements of the Carolinas and Georgia were of English descent, others came from France, Holland, Germany, Sweden, Ireland, and Scotland, as well as dozens of other points of origin. Africans also became part of the New World mix of peoples when they landed here by force during the early 17th century.

The experiences of these colonists along the Atlantic Coast constitutes, in a way, the first of the American frontiers. They built homes in the wilderness, whether they were gold-seeking gentlemen in Jamestown, or pious Pilgrims in Plymouth, or Salzburg Jews in North Carolina. These early immigrants experienced hard times, including food shortages, disease, discouragement, Indian attack, and hostility from other Europeans. But cling they did, and together they formed the basis for what was to develop as a largely Anglo-American population in North America.

The term *Anglo-American* refers to the large majority of immigrants to the original thirteen colonies along the Atlantic Coast who came from the British Isles, including England, Wales, and Scotland. America's roots lay in English traditions, customs, laws, institutions, and arts.

For over a century and a half, these first colonists remained close to the Atlantic Coast, rarely venturing out to the unknown west, where Indians remained in significant numbers, and the extensive range of ridges called the Appalachian Mountains stood in the way of progress into the interior.

Moving west, however, was just a matter of time. As more and more people settled in the thirteen colonies, land became less available, causing increasing numbers of settlers to look to the West.

Review and Write

What differences in time and place are given here concerning two American frontier eras?

Early Native American Trails

One of the disincentives to moving west during most of the colonial period in America was the lack of transportation routes into the interior. A look at the topography of the eastern region between the coast and the Appalachians begins to tell the story. Take Virginia for example. Looking at the map, one sees several rivers flowing across the colony from the Appalachians, running east to the Atlantic Ocean. A closer look shows that in many cases, these river parallel one another, generally flowing in a southeasterly direction. This natural reality impacted colonial travel in two specific ways.

For one, it impeded the movement of people from north to south. To travel by land from, say, Jamestown, Virginia, to the next colony north, Maryland, would require the crossing of several significant rivers, including the James, the York, the Rappahannock, and the Potomac, as well as lesser ones. Since there were no bridges across any major river in the colonies, land travel was slow, tedious, and dangerous.

In addition, the roads in the colonies were few and far between. Nearly all of the land between the Appalachians and the coast was forest land, with each acre covered with hundreds of trees, ranging from maples to oaks to chestnuts. Many such trees might measure as much as 10 to 15 feet in circumference. Before roads could be built, these trees had to be removed, a process involving great labor. What roads that did exist were typically nothing more than long stretches of hard-packed earth, which became muddy and rutted with wagon and carriage tracks during rainy seasons. Travel on such roads was often a choice between breathing clouds of dust or getting stuck in mud, ankle deep.

The second impact on colonial movement brought about by the eastern flowing rivers was the natural tendency to move to the west between rivers, rather than across them. Thus, from the outset, the geography of the Atlantic region did encourage some movement west.

Further facilitating this westward movement were Indian trails which ran toward the Appalachians and beyond into the Ohio River Valley. During the 1600s, approximately 300,000 American Indians lived between the Atlantic Ocean and the Mississippi River, over 1000 miles to the west. For centuries, these Native Americans had tramped all over their lands, often following early buffalo trails. Over time, these Indians developed trails of their own, creating paths often no wider than 12 to 18 inches across. Warriors following such paths often moved in single file, as generations of moccasins wore ruts a foot deep along these early American routes.

Such trails typically followed the best routes between destinations. They cut around river bends, avoided the tops of hills (to avoid being seen by an enemy), opened up to meadows thick with wildlife, or even crossed other paths. It was at the junction of such paths that Indians often met to trade between tribes. Later, they met at such places to negotiate with European traders.

Several of these Indian trails would be used by European colonists as they moved into the American interior. In the north, the Iroquois Trail ran from the Hudson River west, flanking the Mohawk River to Lake Erie, across modern-day New York. To the south, the Kittanning Path ran from eastern Pennsylvania across the Appalachians through Kittanning Gorge. Beyond the mountains, the Kittanning reached the Allegheny River, which became the headwaters of the Ohio River. Further south, the Warriors' Path ran from North Carolina to Ohio. One branch of this trail extended as far west as modern-day St. Louis.

Review and Write

1. Describe a typical Eastern Indian trail.

2. Some Native American trails were adopted and adapted by Europeans once they arrived in the New World. Provide examples of two such trails.

Carving New Trails West

The trails established by Native Americans allowed them to travel great distances on foot. The amount of ground covered by Indian runners was phenomenal. Warrior parties could typically cover 100 miles a day, its members running perhaps non-stop. Iroquois men, using their trail systems to the west, raided as far away as South Dakota's Black Hills, a distance of 1500 miles.

While native paths and trails were used by colonists moving into the lands west of their coastal settlements, some trails were carved by Anglo-Americans, as well. Most such roads were carved out to connect the small colonial towns which dotted the landscape with one another.

As early as 1639, Puritan leaders in Massachusetts decided to built a road from the Pilgrims' settlement at Plymouth to the growing town of Boston. But such a road was narrow, little more than a foot trail. In colonial Virginia, which was home to 60,000 people by 1689, additional interior roads were under construction. In some cases, they amounted to no more than a widening of an Indian path. In fact, not until the mid-18th century did any serious road building in America begin to take place.

In the 1750s, the British built two significant frontier roads. To bolster the British claim to the Ohio River Valley, west of the Appalachians, British forces went to war against the French in 1755. A large British army, led by General Edward Braddock, marched into the western wilderness of Virginia and Pennsylvania, following a trading company trail which had been carved out only three years earlier. Braddock's axemen made the road wider and longer, improving the trail considerably. In time, they extended this colonial route as far as Fort Duquesne (later renamed Fort Pitt), located at the headwaters of the Ohio River. Fifty years later, a portion of this road was incorporated into the building of the National Road, the main thorough-fare through the Appalachians and across the Old Northwest territories of Ohio, Indiana, and Illinois.

Three years later, in 1758, another British army

cut a second frontier road across western Pennsylvania. Led by General John Forbes, 1,400 of his 6,500-man force hacked a road out of the wilderness from Lancaster, Pennsylvania, located west of Philadelphia, to Fort Duquesne. For the next 30 years, Forbes's Road was the most widely used land route from the East into the Ohio River Valley. By the 1790s, great freight wagons called Conestogas, built by Germans living in the Conestoga Valley, used the road, with each wagon carrying several tons of goods, supplies, and items for trade.

Forbes's Road and Braddock's Road provided migrants moving into the American interior additional choices for travel. Within just a few years, thousands of settlers, hungry for western land in the Ohio Country poured into that fertile valley. As future decades passed, these roads were further improved and widened.

Once pioneers moved into the Ohio Country, they encountered additional Indian trails that took them further west. The Lake Shore Trail extended from Fort Niagara to Fort Detroit. The Great Trail ran from Fort Pitt to Detroit as well. Another route, the Scioto Trail, covered ground from Lake Erie down into Kentucky and Tennessee. Spurs of this trail included the Scioto-Beaver Trail and the Scioto-Monongahela Trail. Finally, the Venango Trail ran north-south from Presque Isle on Lake Erie to Fort Pitt.

West to the Piedmont

By the second half of the 1600s, those colonists living in the Tidewater region of Virginia had developed a society and New World existence mature enough to expand into the lands to the west, vast acreage away from the Atlantic Coast. So, intrepid settlers began moving into the uplands of the Piedmont and the Great Valley of the Appalachians.

The Piedmont is a plateau lying directly east of the Appalachian Mountains. As early as 1671, colonial explorers from Virginia first penetrated the region, moving along the Blue Ridge, the eastern-most hill line of the Appalachians. There they discovered the New River which flowed into the Great Kanawha River, which in turn served as a tributary of the Ohio River.

The early colonial explorers settled in the Piedmont plateau, establishing bases of operation along the Fall Line. This natural alteration in the landscape serves as the dividing line between the Tidewater lands of eastern Virginia and the Piedmont itself. The line marks the locales along the various rivers that flow east from the Appalachians and take a sharp tumble as rapids and even waterfalls. Several key American cities had already been established along the Fall Line, and others would come later—New York City, Philadelphia, Baltimore, Washington, DC, Richmond (VA), Raleigh (NC), Columbia (SC), and Macon (GA).

Along the Fall Line, colonists began building a series of trading posts. These forts served as places where Indians could bring their furs and other peltry to trade for European goods, including metal axes, cooking pots, and muskets. The most significant of these Piedmont forts was Fort Henry, established in 1645 along the Fall Line of the Appomattox River, a tributary of the James River.

For decades, these forts sent out brave traders across the Piedmont and into the backcountry of Virginia and the Carolinas to trade with the Native Americans. Pack trains of 100 or more horses annually made the trek through the mountains carrying trade goods into the interior and returning with deerskins and other furs. Such trade into the Piedmont frontier continued through the 1600s and well into the 1700s.

While the early Piedmont fur trade provided an economic base for westward movement into the region, other economic activities came later. The second economic phase in the region was based in cattle. Virginia "cowboys" raised half-wild steers and horses, establishing an early form of the cattle industry which would develop on the Great Plains of the West by the 1860s. These cattlemen used some of the same techniques used in the 19th century on western ranches, including annual spring roundups and cattle branding.

The third stage of development in the Piedmont frontier was the settling of pioneer farmers, especially Germans. Many of them moved into the region after 1720, when a Virginia law opened up 1000-acre tracts of free land to any and all who would settle on the frontier counties of Virginia, with Indians still in close proximity. Later groups of Germans, many of them Mennonites, also settled in the region, lured by literature advertising William Penn's colony as a haven in the New World.

Others who came to the region were the Scot-Irish, men and women who were actually Scots by blood but had migrated to America from settlements in the Ulster counties of Ireland. They arrived in the portion of the Piedmont located in western Pennsylvania.

Review and Write

1. Identify the three stages of economic movement west into the Piedmont region of Virginia and the Carolinas.

2. Once early colonists established themselves along the Atlantic Coast of Virginia, they then moved further west into the Piedmont region. Describe the location and topography of the Piedmont.

Frontier Protection

By 1725, most of the choice locations for settlements east of the Appalachians had been grabbed up by the first of the settlers moving west from the Atlantic Coastal lands. Throughout western Pennsylvania and the northern portion of western Virginia (the modern-day state of West Virginia), little available land remained.

This caused many new settlers and even some of the old, restless ones to move south into southern Virginia and the Carolinas in search of land for their homes and farms. Many such would-be settlers were poor, unable to pay much for western land. Often, even those who purchased land remained unclear where exactly their acres were located, since they had few maps and almost no accurate surveys. As a result, the settlement patterns were usually confusing, and land claims overlapped.

One incentive for moving into western Virginia was the colonial law recognizing the right of landless settlers, often called "squatters," to claim a "cabin right." This privilege allowed anyone who raised a cabin and planted at least one acre of corn to claim 400 acres of available Virginia property.

This type of incentive brought thousands of settlers into the interior eager to make their homes in the wilderness, just as earlier generations of Europeans had settled along the Atlantic Coast in the early 1600s.

Such lands were still home to eastern Indian tribes, however. Tribes such as the Cherokee lived in eastern South Carolina and northern Georgia. Their presence, as well as the presence of other tribes caused western settlers to establish communities designed for protection.

A typical settlement pattern might involve 50 or 60 cabins, each providing a home for a family or two. The cabins were built along five or ten miles of a local river, which provided the pioneers with fresh water. In the midst of their settlement, the frontier Piedmont settlers built a blockhouse for protection.

Blockhouses were similar to the one shown on this page. They were frontier fortresses against hostile Indians. Sometimes they stood alone while others were built as part of a stockade wall, located typically at a corner. Large forts might feature more than one blockhouse.

They were formidable buildings. Usually two-story structures, they were erected out of logs and carefully built for stability. Their logs were hewn flat on both top and bottom so they would fit snugly together to keep out stray shots and arrows. Their horizontal logs were notched at the corners and cut so that logs fit as tightly as possible.

The first floor of the typical blockhouse measured 20 by 30 feet along its outside wall. The first floor ceiling was about 12 feet high. The second floor ceiling was less high, about eight feet. The second story room was larger, however, since the outer walls were built to hang out about two or three feet from the walls of the first story.

Inside these defensive walls, the frontier settlers would gather for protection. The blockhouse had only one outside door and defenders gained access to the second story by a ladder which extended through a trap door cut into the first floor ceiling. Blockhouses might include fireplaces or even a well dug under the ground floor. In the walls of the fortification, the pioneers cut loopholes about two feet apart on all four sides of the structure. These openings were usually three inches wide and designed to allow frontier marksmen to fire their muskets and rifles against all intruders.

A blockhouse could be defended indefinitely unless the enemy managed to set the building's roof on fire or those inside were starved into submission before anyone from the outside could rescue them.

The Ohio Valley Rivalries

As more and more English colonists pushed their way west, crossing the various chains and ridges of the Appalachian Mountains, a clash developed between the two dominant European powers in North America: Great Britain and France. For generations, the French had occupied Canada, had traded for furs with the Native Americans, established scattered settlements of farmers, fur trappers, and powerful landowners. During the 1600s, French explorers, including Champlain, Marquette and Joliet, and La Salle had tramped the backcountry of the Ohio River Valley, crisscrossed the Great Lakes, and staked claims on behalf of the French Empire in America.

By the 1750s, the French were busy building a series of forts, some of them massive stone structures, along the eastern Great Lakes and significant rivers of the northern Trans-Appalachian region, locating them directly in the path of English colonial immigrants. They were concerned that their scattered settlements, such as Detroit, Vincennes, and Kaskaskia were vulnerable in their isolation. Since Great Britain claimed these same lands, it was inevitable the two powers would go to war.

By 1754, French forts lined the southern banks of Lake Erie, and continued in a line to the south to the junction of the Allegheny and Monongahela rivers, which formed the headwaters of the Ohio River. There, they would build Fort Duquesne. This fortress provided the French with a block to English advancement into Ohio and their access to the Ohio River. The British in America would not stand by and watch this part of the frontier close to them.

The approaching clash of arms was not to be limited to just the French, the British, and their colonial counterparts in America. The Ohio Country was home to many tribes of Native Americans who also had a stake in the outcome of any frontier conflict between European superpowers. Tribes from the Northeast had fled to the Ohio Country under the crush of increasing numbers of colonists in New England, New York,

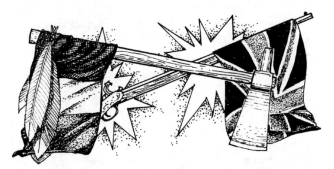

and Pennsylvania. The Delawares, Shawnees, Hurons, and Iroquois were among the most significant nations now watching the French and British closely. Many of these "Ohio tribes" wanted to see the British advancement into the western frontier stopped and the lands left open for Indian occupation. They were also opposed to the movement of the French into the same region.

As war approached, the Iroquois Confederacy (which included the Mohawk, Cayuga, Seneca, Tuscarora, Oneida, Onondaga tribes) attempted to maintain a policy of neutrality. However, Iroquois splinter factions allied themselves with either the British or the French.

The approaching conflict, known as the French and Indian War, began in 1755 with the advancement of a British army into the wilderness of western Pennsylvania. Led by General Edward Braddock, and bound for Fort Duquesne, Braddock's army was ambushed by a handful of French Canadians and many Indian allies. Braddock himself was killed and his army destroyed. (A young George Washington participated in the Battle of the Wilderness as a Virginia colonial militia officer.)

Braddock's defeat was followed by the outbreak of full-scale war between the French and the British by 1756. The first two years of the conflict went badly for the British, who were regularly defeated in the field and lost a string of their own forts in northern New York. Indian allies of the French raided English colonial settlements, killing thousands of colonists on the frontier. For the time being, the fate of the Ohio Country frontier hung in the balance.

The Fight for the Ohio

Great Britain's military efforts in America during the first few years of the French and Indian War were generally unsuccessful. Forts fell, including Fort Oswego, on the banks of Lake Ontario and Fort William Henry, situated on Lake George in northern New York. (Decades later, American author James Fenimore Cooper included the fall of William Henry and the massacre which followed in his classic frontier romance, *The Last of the Mohicans*.)

But, by 1758, the British turned the war around, thanks to the recommitment to the New World conflict by a newly appointed British prime minister, William Pitt. Pitt committed more than 20,000 British regulars to the colonial conflict, helping create an army of 50,000 men, including colonial militiamen.

In addition, the British lured Indian support for their cause, promising them they would take into consideration "the grievances complained of by the Indians, with respect to the lands which have been fraudulently taken from them. By 1758, British officials promised the Iroquois Confederacy and the Ohio Indians that Great Britain would, after the French and Indian War, establish a fixed border between English settlements on the frontier and the hunting grounds of the Native Americans.

With renewed commitment, the British began turning the war around, capturing a series of French forts, including Louisburg in the summer of 1758. By 1759, the British captured Forts Niagara, Saint Frederec, and Carillon, with the Fort Carillon campaign involving 12,000 British regulars. By summer's end, the strategic site of Quebec had fallen to the British, and French Montreal was in British hands by 1760.

Having triumphed in the course of the war, the British extracted a harsh treaty from the French. The Treaty of Paris (1763) ceded all of French Canada to the British, ending the significant European rivalry over the Ohio Country.

But international struggles over this much desired region were not completely over. When the Ohio Indians realized the French had lost their efforts to take control of the region, they were stunned, believing it was not theirs to lose or to grant to the British. And new British policies shocked these tribes of Native Americans even more. The British general, Jeffrey Amherst, now British military governor of the western region, banned the old policy of giving presents as peace tokens to the Indian chiefs and tribes of the frontier. He also banned all trade with Native Americans involving guns and ammunition. This infuriated and frustrated the Ohio tribes since they had become accustomed, even dependent, on such trade and gifts from both the French and British.

These policy changes made life difficult for these tribes. Frontier conflict continued after the French and Indian War as a Delaware leader named Neolin (his name meant "The Enlightened One" in Algonquian) began to rally hundreds of warriors against the English. A confederacy of chiefs came together as followers of the prophet Neolin, among them an Ottawa leader named Pontiac. During the spring and summer of 1763, Pontiac led an Indian uprising, inspired by the words of Neolin, and established in the belief that the time was right for the Native Americans of Ohio to rally together and resist the colonial expansion of the British and their colonists into the Ohio frontier.

Off and on, over the next decade, the Ohio frontier was a violent place, rocked by recurring Indian struggles against English encroachment; it was to be a time of killing, even massacres, as the future of the region remained in question.

Review and Write

1. During the French and Indian War, the British convinced various Native American tribes to side with them against the French. What kinds of promises did the British make to gain loyalty?

2. Once the British won the war, how did they treat the Native Americans who had helped them?

Pontiac's Rebellion

The summer of 1763 witnessed renewed violence on the Ohio frontier. The Ottawa chief, Pontiac, led a coalition of tribes against the British presence in the west, making a regular practice of attacking western forts along the Great Lakes, some of them former French outposts where these same Indians had traded prior to the French and Indian War.

When warriors attacked the British fort Michilimackinac, located at the narrows between lakes Michigan and Huron, they pretended to be playing a ball game similar to lacrosse outside the fort. British soldiers watched unsuspectingly, cheering the Indian players as a ball rolled into the fort with the Indian athletes in hot pursuit. Only then did the warriors turn to their true business of killing British soldiers, plus others inside the British fortification.

All across the Ohio backcountry, the killing raged through the 1763 summer, resulting in the murders of over 2000 English subjects. Eight British forts fell to the Native Americans, which were subsequently looted and burned. General panic reigned among western settlements.

General Jeffrey Amherst, from his base headquarters at Fort Pitt (the former French Fort Duquesne), suggested that his officers should combat the violence by spreading smallpox throughout the warring tribes by distributing blankets infected disease's germs. Serious smallpox epidemics developed, spreading through the Delawares and Shawnees and further south to the Creeks, Choctaws, and Chickasaws. Hundreds of Native Americans died of the dreaded disease.

Pontiac's Rebellion continued into 1764, but, despite the success of Native American wars, they failed to bring about the collapse of Forts Niagara, Detroit, or Pitt. After a year, many of Pontiac's allies gave up their efforts, afraid their villages and families would be targeted by the British for destruction. By the rebellion's end, 4000 British colonists and regular troops had been killed.

By 1764, the war between the Native Americans of the Ohio Country stalled out into stalemate. The revolt had solved little. Yet British authorities pursued a new policy toward the Indians, one which had actually been enacted by Parliament prior to the outbreak of Pontiac's Rebellion. Through the Royal Proclamation of 1763, the British set off the lands west of the Appalachians as an "Indian Reserve," a region which was to be left for occupation by Native Americans.

Ultimately, this proclamation was just the policy the Indians of the Ohio Country had been looking for. But colonial immigrants, land speculators, and the residents of British forts in the west were angered by the proclamation. They had hoped that, with the removal of the French in the region, those western lands would be open to settlement by British colonists.

So much bitterness accompanied the colonial response to the Proclamation of 1763 that a mob of frontiersmen in Pennsylvania known as the Paxton Boys, raided an Indian settlement, slaughtering 20 native men, women, and children living in the village of Conestoga along the banks of the Susquehanna River in December of 1763. When colonial officials attempted to arrest members of the Paxton Boys, 600 Pennsylvania frontiersmen rallied behind the murderers. Only through the negotiating efforts of Benjamin Franklin, respected Philadelphia printer and colonial leader, was future violence defused.

Despite the efforts and official policy of the British Crown, American pioneers continued to pour into the Ohio Country, despite the Proclamation of 1763. The tide of western migration, of movement and settlement along the Trans-Appalachian frontier was well on its way.

Review and Write

1. Given the Proclamation of 1763, why was Pontiac's Rebellion somewhat needless?

2. What secret weapon did General Jeffrey Amherst use against the Native Americans?

——Into the Trans-Appalachian West——

Following the French and Indian War, a victorious Great Britain looked to the west and saw problems in the future for its American colonies. Colonists were already moving through the Appalachians, lured by the possibilities of rich land in Ohio or Kentucky. Parliament, to discourage such movement, passed the Proclamation of 1763, which closed off the lands west of the mountains to colonial migration as an Indian reserve for the Native Americans of the region, some of whom had been driven from their ancestral homes along the Atlantic Coast by earlier generations of European settlers.

However, no paper law could keep would-be pioneers from making the trek through the mountains to the western lands. In fact, the greatest impediment to western movement was not an unenforceable English law, but the topography of the land itself. The real barrier to advancement across the land was the Appalachian Mountains.

The Appalachians are actually three chains of mountains, not one. They lie along a northeast to southeast parallel, with each chain presenting its own set of obstacles to west-bound pioneers. The first obstacle was the Blue Ridge Mountains, which extended all the way from Pennsylvania to Georgia, a long, snaking single high ridge marked the upper extension through Pennsylvania and Virginia. But the ridge fanned out to the south into the Great Smoky Mountains in Tennessee and the Carolinas.

Beyond the Blue Ridge lay the linear ridges, or parallel ridges of the Appalachians. These represented some of the tallest mountains of the region, rising some 4000 feet from the valley floor. To the west stood the Allegheny Front. This extensive front runs from New York, highlighted by the Catskill Mountains, then continues to Alabama. This ridge is steep, and, for many an 18th-century pioneer, represented the most difficult portion of an Appalachian crossing.

In combination, these three chains gave the settlers a serious challenge. The problem was in finding an opening through all three chains. An opening in one chain, often called a "gap," did not typically line up with an opening in the next range, causing the settlers to have to move laterally through river choked valleys in search of another opening in the next ridge.

Some connecting gaps were discovered, however, in the southern portion of the mountain chains. In the Blue Ridge, it is the Saluda Gap, taking pioneers into the valley of the French Broad River, which provided the second gap. The third is the Cumberland Gap, which passes through the Cumberland Escarpment located on the border between the western lands of Tennessee and Kentucky.

But even when pioneers knew of the gaps, there was an ongoing problem with Indians. These mountain passes were blocked by various tribes and the Saluda-Cumberland Gap was sometimes controlled by the Shawnee, a fierce tribe with which to contend.

By the mid-18th century, the Shawnee abandoned the region and migrated north across the Ohio River, allowing for greater movement of Anglo-Americans through the mountains and into Kentucky.

There, the Blue Grass region awaited, a place thick with oak, hickory, and chestnut trees. In the 1750s, it was unoccupied by Indians. In addition, the land of meadows and open fields, some of which had been cleared by generations of Indians, was home for an abundance of wildlife. Here, too, and elsewhere in Kentucky, the numerous salt deposits, known as "licks," served as a constant lure for animals and men alike.

Early Land Speculation

While central Kentucky was not home to any Indian tribes during the 1750s and '60s, this was only true in a technical sense. In reality, Indians roamed the region regularly, as hunters from different tribes—Miamis, Fox, Sauk, Shawnee, and others—causing recurring clashes and short-lived raids and wars. The land, a scene of violence, became known as an Indian no-man's-land. To many, it was known as "the dark and bloody ground."

As whites moved into the region, migration occurred in stages. The first stage consisted of hunters and trappers. One of the first was Dr. Thomas, who discovered the Cumberland Gap in 1750. Close behind him came Christopher Gist, who, also in 1750, explored nearly all of Kentucky as far as the Miami River. Two years later, John

Finley arrived at the site of the Falls of the Ohio River, near where Louisville, Kentucky, stands today. (Finley would later have a direct influence on such famous Kentucky personalities as Daniel Boone, after the two men met in 1755.) In some respects, men such as Daniel Boone, who reached the Blue Grass region of Kentucky in 1769, would be late-comers to the West.

The second phase of non-Indians to arrive in Kentucky and Tennessee consisted of land speculators. They often arrived in a region ahead of a great influx of immigrants to establish ownership over huge tracts of land which they sold at a profit through the formation of a land speculation company.

One of the earliest of the western land speculation companies was the Ohio Company, which turned its eyes on Kentucky in 1748. Through petitioning the Virginia government, the Ohio Company gained the rights to 200,000 acres of land located at the forks of the Ohio River and to the south.

Additional land companies followed, but one of the most successful was not formed until 1769, with the development of the Grand Ohio Company. Backed by a group of Pennsylvania investors, this company was large enough to acquire control of other speculation companies, including the Ohio Company. Initially, the Grand Ohio attempted to receive ownership of 20 million acres of eastern Kentucky and western Virginia, a tract to be named Vandalia.

Speculators intended to establish a wide-reaching transmountain colony, but by the time its organizers received permission to establish their Appalachian colony, the American Revolution had begun, bringing an end to British and American cooperation on all levels.

With the Vandalia project stalled, another land speculation project was just getting underway. A North Carolina judge named Richard Henderson, was the mover and shaker in the formation of a North Carolina-based company called the Transylvania Company. Henderson was in communication with Daniel Boone who had visited the region of the Blue Grass. Henderson organized his company in 1774 and, through hard negotiations with the Cherokee Indians, purchased the immense tract of Transylvania for 10,000 pounds.

This purchase was illegal, of course, since the Proclamation of 1763 had closed Kentucky and other western lands to Anglo-American settlement. Henderson bypassed Parliament and British authority altogether, however, appealing to the new American Congress to validate his claim. Congress never did. But Henderson continued with his efforts, finally employing Daniel Boone to take colonists across the mountains.

Daniel Boone's Early Years

Few American school children have not heard of the famous frontiersman and trailblazer, Daniel Boone. As famous an individual as can be found in American history, Daniel Boone represents the essence of the pioneering spirit found in America in the 1700s. His efforts at establishing settlements in Kentucky and building the pioneer trail known as the Wilderness Road form the core of this hardy explorer's contribution to the frontier experience.

Boone was born on November 2, 1734, in a Pennsylvania log cabin situated along the banks of the Schuylkill River, near modern-day Reading. His parents were Quakers, and his father operated a small farm, as well as a blacksmith shop. When Daniel was only 10 years old, he was kept busy tending cows and learning the ways of the woods. With friendly Indians living close by, young Boone learned how to survive in the wild, how to track animals, plus other frontier skills.

His father provided him with his first rifle when Daniel was only 12. He developed a natural skill for the hunt and developed a sharp eye and a quickness with a gun.

By 1750, his father decided to move into the frontier region of North Carolina, along the Yadkin River. Daniel provided the family with wild game, while his father and brothers farmed. To keep himself supplied with shot and powder, Daniel traded the animal pelts for such supplies.

When Daniel was 20, he joined other back-woodsmen on General Braddock's march in the Wilderness toward Fort Duquesne in 1755. During this campaign against the French, Boone served as a wagon driver. While on this expedition, young Boone met men who had crossed the Appalachians and explored the lands known as Kentucky. One such western veteran was John Finley, who described Kentucky meadows as a wildlife haven— a hunter's paradise, thick with deer, bison, and turkeys, which Finley claimed were so great in number they could not all fly simultaneously without darkening the sky.

From such stories, Boone developed a keen desire to visit Kentucky. Following Braddock's defeat, Boone returned to his father's farm in North Carolina. The next year, Daniel married a 17-year-old neighbor girl named Rebecca Bryan, who was nearly as handy with a rifle as was Boone himself. This union produced nine children.

As the Boone family grew, Daniel was forced to remain at home providing for his wife and children. He still primarily hunted and did little farming. His dreams continued to be filled with aspirations of visiting Kentucky. Then, during the winter of 1768, a peddler arrived at the Boone cabin, selling housewares and other goods. It proved to be John Finley, whom Boone immediately recognized. Finley, once again, talked up the hunting opportunities to be found in Kentucky. He informed Daniel of a route leading through the Appalachians, called the Warriors' Path.

Boone could no longer contain his desire to see Kentucky. He convinced a brother-in-law, John Stuart and a few other brave souls to go with him and, in 1769, the small party set out for the western unknown. One of Boone's brothers, Squire, joined the party later.

Moving across the Piedmont region just east of the Appalachians, Boone and his party found the Warriors' Trail, which was a narrow but long-used path. The route took the men through the Cumberland Mountains, passing along the Cumberland Gap and into the rich, western lands of Kentucky. There, all Finley's stories about game in abundance proved true, as Boone and his men relished in hunting everything from bison to turkeys.

Review and Write

1. What role did the frontiersman John Finley play in convincing young Daniel Boone to go west into Kentucky?

2. What experiences from youth prepared Daniel Boone for a life on the frontier?

The Kentucky Trailblazer

Typically, Daniel Boone is pictured as a frontiersman, big in stature, wearing a coonskin cap, and brandishing a Pennsylvania rifle. This picture is only partially accurate. Boone was, in fact, not a tall man at all, and he did not wear a coonskin, but rather a felt hat. He did carry a Kentucky rifle, as well as a tomahawk and a knife.

He wore a deerskin outfit, which included a fringed hunting shirt that extended to his knees, as well as deerskin leggings and leather moccasins. Across his shoulder, Boone carried a leather pouch filled with lead bullets and small cloth patches that were used when loading a frontier musket, as well as a powder horn of gunpowder. His black felt hat was pulled over his dark, coarse hair that he kept long, tying it back in a pigtail, called a queue.

Boone's wanderlust had led him to Kentucky in 1769, where he and his fellow trailblazers hunted huge herds of Eastern bison, turkey, and deer that grazed in the natural meadowlands of fertile Kentucky valleys. Boone remained in this hunter's paradise for two years before returning home to his family.

During such absences, his wife, Rebecca, tended her family and waited for her husband's return. She was a courageous woman who always hoped Daniel would return alive and in one piece. Rebecca kept the family farm operating.

When Boone finally returned from his first trip to Kentucky, he was ready to move his family across the Appalachians. In 1773, the Boone family and several others, set out for Kentucky, only to turn back after Indians attacked the party, killing Boone's oldest son, James. Two years would pass before Boone attempted a return to Kentucky.

Then, in 1775, Boone was hired by a North Carolina judge named Richard Henderson to lead a group of settlers to Kentucky where they would receive land purchased from Henderson's land company, the Transylvania Company. Henderson's dream was to build a Kentucky colony. Boone blazed an extensive trail system through the frontier and the Appalachians to Kentucky which became known as the Wilderness Road. Over the following decades, thousands of pioneers used this route to reach Tennessee and Kentucky.

After leading Henderson's colonists to Kentucky, Boone established a settlement along the Kentucky River, called Boonesborough, where Lexington, Kentucky stands today. Boone's family followed him across the mountains and settled with the party in Henderson's colony, which was given the name Transylvania. The Native Americans in the region did not accept their presence and Indian attacks occurred more than once.

In 1778, Boone himself was captured by Shawnee Indians, who tortured him, yet took him into their tribe, noting his bravery. Boone remained with the Indians until he heard of their plans to attack Boonesborough. He managed to warn the settlers before the attack took place.

Boone spent the next 20 years leading settlers into Kentucky, surveying property, and claiming land for himself. Because he failed to properly file his land claims, Boone later lost all his land in Kentucky, prompting him to move further west, to Spanish Missouri. In 1799, Boone settled 40 miles west of St. Louis in the Femme Osage district. Local Spanish officials appointed the famous frontiersman as a local judge. Ironically, when the land became part of the United States in 1803, Boone again lost his property. By 1814, however, the U.S. Congress granted land to Boone, then 80 years old, for his service on the frontier which had "opened the way for millions of his fellow men."

The Watauga Settlements

While Judge Richard Henderson's Transylvania Company attempted to sell land to would-be pioneers to Kentucky, other land companies were attempting to lure pioneers to other portions of the Trans-Appalachian West.

One such effort was mounted by the Loyal Land Company in western Virginia. Between 1750 and 1754, frontier families purchased land from Loyal in the middle of the Appalachian region. Settlements were established in the Powell and Holston Valleys east of the Cumberland Gap. The Holston and Powell were tributary rivers of the Tennessee River.

Following the Seven Years' War, between 1768 and 1773, the next generation of pioneers in the region pushed further down the Holston, laying out new sites for settlement. Still others occupied lands adjacent to yet another river in the region, the French Broad, a tributary of the Holston, located to the east. These settlements were known as the Watauga Settlements.

Local government among these settlements took the form of the Watauga Association, a group of early settlers who, in 1772, drew up the first written constitution in North America. Among their leaders were John Sevier and James Robertson, one of the founders of Nashville (originally called Fort Nashborough).

About this same time, men such as Daniel Boone were moving settlers into Kentucky, where the big push came in 1780. Three years later, there were between 15,000 and 20,000 settlers in the Blue Grass region.

Paralleling that movement was a migration of Trans-Appalachian settlers bound for another Blue Grass region—this one located in central Tennessee. The Nashville Basin received its first flock of pioneer farmers in 1779. By the end of the Revolutionary War (1783), the number of settlers in central Tennessee numbered between 25,000 and 30,000. Considering the events that were taking place and considering the number of Indians still roaming in the same region, this growth was substantial and swift,

What factors caused this great influx of pioneers into Tennessee? Several are clear. The area was ideal for farming, with the land rich and fertile, and the climate advantageous for a lengthy growing season. Also, access to Tennessee was easier by road by the late 1770s. Such interior highways as Braddock's Road, which connected the Potomac River with the Ohio, and Forbes's Road, which extended from Philadelphia to the forks of the Ohio River were in place by 1758. Other routes helped deliver thousands of settlers into Tennessee as well. In the southern portion of the Appalachians, the Wilderness Trail provided a viable route. While the trail was little more than a packhorse path prior to the 1790s, it was widened and became a regular road by 1796.

Two significant regional groups followed the Wilderness Trail to Tennessee. One came out of Pennsylvania and Maryland, while the other originated in the Carolina Piedmont. Both groups used the Saluda-Cumberland Gap access.

A third factor leading to rapid occupation of Tennessee was the availability of inexpensive land during the Revolutionary War. Pioneers could purchase land as cheaply as 25 cents an acre. In addition, veterans of the Revolutionary War came to Tennessee by the thousands, granted free land by the new national government. Privates who had seen three years of military service were granted allotments of 200 acres, while officers received additional acres according to rank. A colonel, for example, was entitled to a grant of 5000 acres of western land.

Review and Write

1. From 1750 through the 1770s, settlers continued to establish new outposts on the frontier. Where were some of these wilderness outposts built?

2. What incentives drew settlers into Tennessee through the 1770s and 1780s?

Test I

Part I.

Matching. *Match the answers shown below with the statements given above. Place the letters of the correct answers in the spaces below.*

1. The first motion picture with a plot, a western, released in 1913
2. Eastern frontier region stretching as far west as the Mississippi River
3. Western frontier region lying west of the Mississippi River and stretching through the Rockies
4. Frontier trail running from the Hudson River west, flanking the Mohawk River to Lake Erie
5. Frontier trail running from North Carolina to Ohio; one branch extended west to St. Louis
6. 1758 frontier road carved by a British general, extending from Lancaster, PA., to Ft. Duquesne
7. Significant frontier outpost in colonial Virginia situated on the Fall Line; used for fur trading
8. Region lying between the Atlantic Coast plain and the Appalachian Mountains
9. Privilege to claim 400 acres of Virginia land after building house and planting an acre of corn
10. Fortification commonly found on the Piedmont frontier to provide protection against Indians
11. By definition, the "frontier" lies between civilization and this place
12. Wagon style used frequently in the American colonies and on the Trans-Appalachian frontier

A. cabin right	B. Iroquois Trail	C. Piedmont	D. wilderness
E. Forbes's Road	F. The Great Train Robbery	G. Trans-Mississippi	H. Fort Henry
I. Warriors' Path	J. blockhouse	K. Trans-Appalachian	L. Conestoga

1. ____ 2. ____ 3. ____ 4. ____ 5. ____ 6. ____ 7. ____ 8. ____ 9. ____ 10. ____ 11. ____ 12. ____

Part II.

Matching. *Match the answers shown below with the statements given above. Place the letters of the correct answers in the spaces below.*

1. Trans-Appalachian region which the French and British both claimed, leading to war
2. French fort located at the confluence of the Monongahela and Allegheny Rivers
3. Union of Indian tribes which included the Mohawk, Cayuga, Seneca, Oneida, and Onondaga
4. British general defeated in eastern Pennsylvania in 1755 by French and Indian forces
5. Native American leader who attempted to rally Indians against the English
6. British general who, after the French and Indian War, banned presents to Indian chiefs
7. Pennsylvanians who led raid against Indians living in village of Conestoga in 1763
8. Parliamentary decree which closed the Trans-Appalachian West to American migration
9. Eastern-most line of Appalachian Mountains
10. Popular opening in Appalachian Mountains used by American immigrants into Kentucky
11. Tract of eastern Kentucky and western Virginia land sought by Grand Ohio Company
12. North Carolina judge who formed the Transylvania Company

A. Braddock	B. Proclamation of 1763	C. Richard Henderson	D. Ohio Valley
E. Duquesne	F. Saluda-Cumberland	G. Paxton Boys	H. Neolin
I. Amherst	J. Iroquois Confederacy	K. Blue Ridge	L. Vandalia

1. ____ 2. ____ 3. ____ 4. ____ 5. ____ 6. ____ 7. ____ 8. ____ 9. ____ 10. ____ 11. ____ 12. ____

Treaties and Warfare

During the 1760s and into the 1770s, the pioneer movement into the western frontier continued on several different fronts. Men such as Daniel Boone helped open up the Trans-Appalachian region of Kentucky while others provided leadership elsewhere.

The British policy based in the Proclamation of 1763, which closed the frontier to colonial migration was generally ignored. Even the British never seemed particularly interested in promoting and backing the policy. Almost before the ink was dry on the original document which intended to halt western migration of Anglo-Americans, the movement was already underway.

New Englanders moved by the thousands into the lands dotted by the northern Green Mountains (in modern-day Vermont). New York migrants encroached onto traditional Iroquois lands. Thousands settled in western Pennsylvania, in and around the strategically located Fort Pitt. A procession of immigrants—hunters, fur traders, cattle herders, and yeoman farmers traveled over the Appalachians, settling in modern-day West Virginia, western Virginia, and the rugged hill country of eastern Tennessee.

Land speculators had a difficult time keeping up with these constant streams of migrating, land-hungry pioneers. Large profits could be made in the buying and selling of western property. Even prominent Virginia plantation owner, George Washington, made attempts to involve himself in land speculation.

In 1768, the Ohio Company sent its representatives and surveyors into the upper Ohio Valley, making ready the way for settlers to claim land under legitimate title. With these influences in the west, the British authorities felt compelled to respond to frontier pressure by negotiating with Native Americans for their lands. They negotiated with the Iroquois and the Cherokees, two nations of Indians holding significant power among native tribes. But they could no longer threaten the British by allying themselves with the French. With no real options left, short of war, such tribes reluctantly signed away portions of their lands.

The Cherokees ceded a large tract of their lands located along the banks of the upper Tennessee River through negotiations which produced the Treaty of Hard Labor in 1768. Later that same year, the Iroquois did the same, surrendering their claim to the Ohio River Valley under the Treaty of Fort Stanwix.

While British authorities representing the Crown typically negotiated with Native Americans,

some colonial leaders were not satisfied with the pace of British policy. In 1774, John Murray, Earl of Dunmore, and governor of Virginia encouraged a war with the Shawnee tribe to gain land from them. Through Dunmore's War, colonial authorities forced the Shawnee to cede their lands in the upper Ohio Country to Virginia.

When other tribes protested the actions taken through Dunmore's War, colonial authorities ignored them. When the Iroquois and the Ohio Indians reminded Governor Dunmore that the British Crown had promised the maintaining of a boundary line between colonial peoples and themselves, Dunmore would not hear any of it.

As one Native American leader put it: "The Americans entirely disregard and despise the settlement agreed upon by their superiors and us." He continued to note that Americans "are coming in vast numbers to the Ohio and [give] our people to understand that they would settle wherever they pleased." But the concerns of the Indians were soon lost as the American Revolution approached.

New Trails Across the Frontier

The efforts of men such as Daniel Boone helped to establish a foothold of Anglo-Americans in the Trans-Appalachian West. By the end of 1775, as the colonies were slipping into the American Revolution, several hundred pioneers traveled Boone's Wilderness Road into Kentucky.

As more and more people used Boone's Wilderness Road, a need arose to develop additional routes and branches throughout the region. As would-be settlers looked south to Tennessee, another route, the Tennessee Path, ran across northern Tennessee. Additional thoroughfares spread across the landscape of Kentucky, connecting and crisscrossing the West. A new route developed, running from the frontier settlement of Louisville, Kentucky, on the Ohio River, west to Vincennes, Indiana, then on to the far western village of St. Louis in Spanish Louisiana (modern-day Missouri).

Even old trails were eventually improved for greater flow of migrants and frontier traffic. In 1795, the Kentucky legislature (Kentucky had become a state in 1792) adopted a bill called "An Act Opening a Wagon Road to Cumberland Gap." The purpose of the act was obvious: To widen the old Indian trail, making it passable for wagons to cross the Cumberland Gap, following Daniel Boone's Wilderness Road all the way to Crab Orchard, Kentucky, nestled in the heart of the state.

North of Kentucky, still other trails were being developed to facilitate the movement of Trans-Appalachian migration. A trail between Baltimore, Maryland, and Redstone, Pennsylvania was developed into a significant wagon road by the 1780s. Extensions of this route included a path leading northwest through the upper Shenandoah Valley, ultimately connecting to the Baltimore-Redstone Trail. These trails served as access roads and paths into another portion of the Trans-Appalachian West: the Ohio Country.

As more and more Americans eyed this rich region, the young United States government helped develop the routes into Ohio. In 1796, President George Washington was authorized by Congress to contract with Ebenezer Zane to establish a trail across Ohio. Zane, a resident of Maryland, began to carve his trail at Wheeling, Virginia (today it is in the state of West Virginia) and into southeast Ohio. The route crossed into the eastern portion of the territory to a site located along the banks of the Muskingum River. There, Zane established a community he called Zanesville. Zane opened a ferry there to bring settlers across the Muskingum River. In time, Zane extended his trail to the Ohio River and the Kentucky River to a settlement called Limestone. Although Zane's Trace was one of the earliest non-Indian trails in Ohio, it would later serve as a portion of a major highway across the frontier, the National Road.

In addition to the establishment of Zane's Trace across Ohio, another significant route west was underway in Pennsylvania. In 1791, construction began on one of the first turnpikes in America, the Lancaster Pike. After six years of construction, the Lancaster route opened to travel in 1797. The pike connected Philadelphia, one of the largest cities in the United States, with Lancaster, Pennsylvania. The Lancaster Pike was a unique road, indeed. In a time when most roads were simply made of dirt, the Lancaster route used crushed rock smaller than one inch in diameter. This stone foundation was laid at least 10 inches deep, and was wide enough to allow two lanes of wagon traffic to pass by one another. This 60-mile-long route was expensive, costing nearly $500,000.

The Conestoga Wagon

As "hard roads" such as the Lancaster Pike came into use, Americans were better able to move into the West. While such roads were built to accommodate all forms of traffic, including wagons, carts, farm animals, and people on horseback and on foot, the Lancaster Pike soon became crowded with a common form of wagon found in frontier Pennsylvania—the Conestoga wagon.

The Conestoga wagon was one of the most extraordinary land vehicles of the 18th century. It was one of the most durable wagons ever built and a pioneer who had one could travel just about anywhere.

Conestoga-like wagons were first built in the European nations of Germany and England. But the original and true "Conestoga" was first made in the Conestoga Valley of Pennsylvania by German immigrants who were master wagon builders. These "Pennsylvania Dutch" became known for their solid craftsmanship and attention to detail, as they designed a wagon of extraordinary capacity and beauty.

The first recorded mention of the Conestoga wagon was made in 1717, when such wagons carried furs from Lancaster to Philadelphia, prior to the building of the Lancaster Pike. In those pre-pike days, the Lancaster route was difficult, requiring four days travel to cover 60 miles. Typically, ordinary wagons would fall apart and collapse under any heavy loads.

But the Conestoga was different. Such wagons carried farm produce and even unusual items, such as bears' oil and honey, with relative ease. They were used to haul iron products such as heavy anvils and farm equipment. Throughout the 18th century, the Conestogas were more and more recognized as the workhorse wagons of the frontier. And their use was never limited to just Pennsylvania. By 1800, Conestoga wagons were in use all across the United States. Once the National Road was opened, approximately 5000 Conestogas could be found using this famous road on any given day.

The design of the Conestoga wagon was a masterpiece of wagon engineering. The Conestoga featured a bed with a curved bottom, with both ends tilted up to keep cargo inside from falling out, especially when rolling up and down hills. The bed itself measured three feet deep, ten feet long and about 3 and a half feet wide. There was no seat on the wagon, which required the wagon master to walk along side the Conestoga or ride one of the wagon's horses.

The Conestoga was a covered wagon, meaning it featured great curved bows of wood that arched over the top of the wagon. These bows were covered with white canvas intended to protect the wagon's contents from damage by rain, hail, or other forces of nature. Many Conestogas sported eight such bows, but some models might boast as many as 16.

Many of the wagons featured a toolbox built onto the left side of the wagon bed. With artistic flair, these boxes might be decorated with wood carvings or flowers, hearts, or even snakes. Behind the wagon a feed trough for horses was hung.

A standard color combination was typically used in painting the Conestogas. The wagon bed was painted bright blue, while the wheels were painted a deep red. These wooden wheels were large, measuring about four inches in width. Conestoga wheels were placed about five feet apart, and the back wheels were larger than the front wheels.

The end result of all this German craftsmanship was a popular frontier wagon capable of hauling several tons of cargo. The wagons were pulled by three, four, or six or more large horses, their harnesses strung with bells that chimed the arrival of the Conestogas in many a frontier town.

Review and Write

What qualities made the Conestoga a widely used wagon through the Trans-Appalachian region?

Essential Frontier Tools

The efforts of men such as Daniel Boone and others who helped deliver men and women, as well as their families into the wilderness of the Trans-Appalachian region were followed up by thousands upon thousands of daring pioneer-settlers ready to make a home for themselves in this new country. A look at daily life for such pioneers reveals an existence always in transition, as families attempted to carve a place out of a land that had never known extensive settlement.

In this primitive world of nature, the Anglo-American settlers hacked and burned the forests, clearing land for farming. The process was slow, for even a hearty farmer armed with a good, sharp axe was typically only able to clear about one acre of forested land a year to make it valuable as a piece of farm land. In addition, the settlers of the Trans-Appalachian West dug out tree stumps and erected their primitive lean-tos and cabin shelters. They erected worm fences to help keep their livestock in check.

Near every site where two roads converged, creating a "crossroads," or at shallow places along rivers, sites where settlers could "ford" a stream, entrepreneurial pioneers built stores, blacksmith shops, blockhouses, churches or schools. The cabins were often temporary and, often within five years, such cabins were out-of-date, having been replaced by brick or clapboard houses, including two-story models, all intended for permanence.

In many places, land was distributed through a checkerboard survey system which helped create natural sites for settlements about every six miles,

about the distance a horse and wagon might be able to cover in three or four hours time.

To build their new places in the wilderness of the Trans-Appalachian region, the pioneers brought with them tools that were considered essential for frontier life. First among these tools was the axe. It was the most basic tool of the frontiersman—one he used to clear land, cut logs for his home, chop firewood to heat his house, cut wood to build fences, and even carve rough, primitive pieces of furniture.

The frontier axe was slightly different from the European model that preceded it. The European axe weighed three pounds, was thin, and carried a bit, or blade, that measured about eight inches in length. It resembled more the medieval executioner's axe than the tool used by Abraham Lincoln to split log rails. The American model was developed in 1740, had a wider poll, or handle, adding weight. The bit was still broad, but it had lost its crescent shape. It was better balanced, with the head placed an inch or two forward of the pounding edge and weighing seven pounds. In skilled hands, this hefty axe could cut through a tree trunk measuring a foot in diameter in less then ten minutes.

A "tool" of second importance was the pioneer rifle. This tool provided protection in the wilderness and a means to provide meat for the frontier table. The typical rifle carried to Kentucky was the *Pennsylvania rifle*—a long rifle noted for its firepower and accuracy. The first such long-barreled, muzzle-loading model was crafted in 1728. Many such rifles were manufactured by skilled German craftsmen living in and around Lancaster, Pennsylvania.

The name *rifle* came from the way in which the gun's barrel was bored, with spiral grooves or *rifles* cut into the barrel. This gave the lead bullets a spin as they exited the fired gun, producing a spinning projectile having greater force, and greater accuracy at a greater distance than a typical unrifled musket, resulting in a deadlier weapon.

Daily Frontier Life

Besides the axe and rifle, several other important tools rounded out the frontier arsenal needed to tame the land and build a home. The mattock, or grubbing hoe, was used to dig out roots and stones from the land. The adze, typically featuring a three-foot long handle with a single long blade set at a right angle, was used to square off logs or to smooth out wooden floors in cabins. A tool similar to the adze was the froe, which was used to make shingles or shakes for a house, with the pioneer pounding the froe into a piece of wood by using a wooden mallet, or froe-club.

Rounding out the "truck," or household items, carried by pioneers into the wilderness were various wedges, mallets, knives, plows, plus a yoke for oxen. There might be an iron pot for cooking, a long-handled skillet, several pottery jugs, and pewter ware, including a mug or two. (Pewter is a metal produced by a combination of copper and tin, and it was used by those who could not afford silverware.) A typical Trans-Appalachian settler carried few non-essential items along primitive mountain passes, so only necessary objects were taken, including simple, yet durable clothing, seed for farming, perhaps a few pieces of furniture, and the family Bible.

When a pioneer arrived in Kentucky or Tennessee, or even in other sites to the north, such as Ohio, he and his family lived as simply as possible. The father and his sons would build a partial shelter, a lean-to, that was only finished on one side—probably the southern exposure. The building of lean-to involved felling small trees and using their trunks to support the shelter. Set about ten feet apart, these poles were forked and each held a log, which was stacked with additional logs laid across them. These logs were then covered over with a layer of bark to keep the rain out. A fire was built for warmth and for cooking, as well as a deterrent to wild animals that might invade the primitive home site. Such half-faced camps were not designed to protect the family in winter, so nearly every spare moment was spent by the

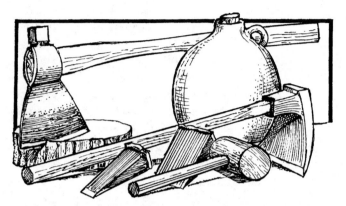

pioneer family in constructing a solid and secure log cabin as quickly as possible.

Most pioneers, if they did not come to Kentucky with hunting skills, soon learned them, in order to provide deer meat, or venison, for hungry families, as well as turkey, squirrel, or duck. If the family maintained chickens, they were eaten on occasion, as well.

The frontier farmer would then set about clearing the trees from a portion of his land. He might use his axe to "girdle" a tree, removing a wide strip of bark completely around the tree, which caused it to die. Within a couple of months, a girdled tree could be dropped, opening up the forest canopy and allowing a patch of sunlight to reach the forest floor. In addition to felling some trees, the pioneer-farmer also cleared the ground of underbrush, vines, and weeds. He planted corn, squash, and beans, the three mainstay crops for Native Americans dating back hundreds of years, and known by the Indians as the "Three Sisters." The corn was not planted in rows as it is today, but rather on small hills, just as the Indians did. Corn, once harvested, could be made into hominy or johnnycakes, or ground into corn meal. Some of the corn might be made into corn liquor, as well.

For several years, the early Trans-Appalachian farmer was a subsistence farmer, producing only enough food for himself and his family. Years might pass before he was able clear more acres of land for farming. After a generation, such a farmer might be planting 50 or 100 acres annually.

Building a Log Cabin

Perhaps no other structure symbolizes the frontier experience in America more than does the log cabin. Early models of this snug, wooden house were actually imported to the American colonies from Sweden. Yet the log cabin today is synonymous with pioneer living.

After a settler moved into a new region and attempted to establish his farm, he would turn to the building of a permanent dwelling, usually a variation on the log cabin. In his early weeks or months on his newly occupied land, the pioneer farmer might live in an open-sided "lean-to," a temporary structure made of tree branches and bark, which left occupants at the mercy of the elements. Otherwise, he and his family might do no better than living inside a wagon or even sleeping outdoors. Building a cabin, then, provided shelter, warmth, security, protection, and permanence.

If such a pioneer had adequate neighbors nearby, there might be a "cabin raising," during which everyone who lived nearby would lend a hand to help build the new cabin. If a settler had no close neighbors, he might have to build the entire structure by himself, using a single axe. Whatever the working circumstances, the materials used in building the cabin had to be available in abundance and within fifteen minutes walking distance of the cabin site itself.

While log cabin designs varied, the typical log cabin was a four-square, with each side relatively equal in length to the other three. The outer walls might be set along the north, south, west, and east points of the compass. The front of the cabin often faced south or east and might either be situated in the midst of a dense eastern forest or along the banks of a river or creek. The cabin, by modern standards, was small, measuring about ten by ten or 20 by 20. Some pioneers built their cabins with dirt floors, while others laid a wooden slab floor.

Building such a cabin required, on average, about 80 logs, approximately 20 per side. About half the logs were fifteen feet in length and the other half, about 20 feet. Log cabins built in New England and on the upper reaches of the Ohio River Valley were often constructed from white pine logs, measuring ten to twelve inches in diameter. Only 50 such logs were needed for such a log cabin. The pioneer farmer dragged his logs to the cabin site behind horses. After stripping the limbs and knots from the logs, while leaving the bark on them, the pioneer used his froe to split some of the better logs and broke others into pieces to make shingles.

As the logs were put in place, forming the outer shape of the cabin, the pioneer used his axe to notch the logs where they would overlap, creating a close bond between the notches. With about 20 logs per side for the typical cabin, the farmer had to devise a method of getting the logs up onto the highest part of each outer wall. A doorway was left in the constructed wall on the front of the log cabin, typically measuring about 40 inches wide and 6 feet high. The door was a wooden slab which was latched on the inside. A crossbar was added for further protection. Such a door would have no knob; only a leather strip attached to the latch. A window or two was included, measuring 18 to 24 inches square.

A fireplace was included on one wall to provide warmth and a cooking site inside the cabin. The early models were made of mud mixed with sticks. Only later were fireplaces constructed out of stone. The spaces between the logs were filled to keep out drafts and the cold. Such spaces were "caulked" with daubing clay, moss, mud mixed with animal hair or straw, as well as small stones and wood chips.

Review and Write

1. What tasks were included in constructing a frontier log cabin?

2. What temporary shelters did pioneers build prior to to the construction of permanent log homes?

Once completed, the pioneer log cabin served the basic needs of the family living in the wilderness of Pennsylvania, Kentucky, or North Carolina. While such small, simple lodgings might seem a compromise to their occupants, it should be remembered that many a pioneer family might have memories of living in Europe where their lives were even more basic. For such a Trans-Appalachian family, the newly finished log cabin was a symbol of their moving up in the world.

Once the cabin was completed, with the logs notched and placed, the roof in order, and a floor established, it was time for the pioneer family to move in. Everything was cozy inside the log cabin. With only one room, no one was ever too distant from fellow family members. Since such houses had no closets or even storage rooms, the walls of the cabin were lined with wooden pegs, from which the frontier family hung their clothes, tools, rifle, and powder horn. A crude, simple shelf held the family's kitchen supplies and utensils.

There would be little furniture in the typical frontier log cabin. Much of it was homemade, carved and hewn by hand. Some pieces were even more simple, such as a 16-inch section of hickory log, standing on end, which served as a block chair. A round, slab of wood was drilled with three holes, which were filled with three pegs, creating a three-legged stool. Two small logs extending from the wall, their ends propped up by two additional log pieces, might provide the framework for a table built into the wall. It would then be covered over with half-faced pieces of wood, making a relatively smooth tabletop. Such simple furniture variations

were endless.

The bed might be a simple wooden frame, set in the corner of the room opposite the fireplace. It might include only one free-standing post, with the other corners attached to the wall itself. The bed "mattress" might consist of nothing more than corn husks or dried leaves covered with a pair of deerhides. If one was lucky, the bed ticking might be filled with feathers. Children would not always have their own beds, but might sleep on the floor near the fireplace hearth.

The first cabin floor was often just dirt, hardpacked with use. In time, a wooden floor might be added. Such floors were typically puncheon, consisting of split logs laid down with the rounded half in the ground, giving at least the illusion of smoothness for the cabin's residents. If the pioneer family had constructed its cabin close to a stone or slate quarry bed, slabs of these stones would be used to cover the bare dirt floor. Here and there the floor, whether dirt, wood, or stone, might be covered over in spots with an animal skin rug.

The next change to the cabin might be the construction of a loft in the house's open attic. The loft rarely covered the entire upper portion of the house, but about one third to a half of the cabin's upper, open space. A ladder might give access to the new attic room, but a more primitive means could be made by drilling a series of vertical holes in the cabin wall, filling them with substantial pegs which could be used to climb into the upper room.

There was no running water or indoor plumbing in frontier homes. Often there was no perceived need for even an outhouse. With few, if any, close neighbors, both women and men would make for the woods when nature called.

Other improvements on the property of the Trans-Appalachian farmer could include the erection of a split rail fence, or a Virginia "worm fence," which would zig-zag its way around the pioneer's land. Such fences corralled the farmer's livestock.

Frontier Alliances, Frontier Wars

While life on the Trans-Appalachian frontier could be rugged, primitive, and even dangerous, tens of thousands of English colonists migrated west of the mountains despite the challenges during the 1760s and '70s. While British land policy could not keep them out, the issue of British opinion was to become second in importance to the colonists once the American Revolution began.

Sparked by issues related to taxation, representation, perceived mistreatment, and a British land policy unpopular with nearly everyone in the colonies, the revolution broke out in the spring of 1775, with the April skirmishes at Lexington and Concord, Massachusetts. While popular patriot rhetoric insisted that Americans were fighting the tyranny of the British Crown, other issues worked their way onto the list of reasons why so many patriots took up arms against England. One of them was western land.

Although those living in the thirteen British colonies had hugged the Atlantic Coast for generations, by the mid-18th century, many were looking to the West, at the lands of the Trans-Appalachian region. Some who supported the revolution dreamed of an America, independent of Britain, which would include not only the thirteen Atlantic colonies, but perhaps Canada and all of the land lying between the Appalachians and the Mississippi, territory which England had gained from France after the French and Indian War.

With this vision in mind, some of the fighting during the Revolutionary War took place in those same places. The Second Continental Congress realized the importance of making alliances with Indian tribes against the British.

The British understood the same thing. Yet the British were much more successful in persuading Indian allies than were the Americans. The western tribes knew that the British had established the Proclamation of 1763, officially closing the Trans-Appalachian region to American settlement. A victory by the Americans against England would mean greater numbers of settlers encroaching on Indian lands. The British drew support from the Cherokees, Creeks, Choctaws, and Chickasaws in the South, arming them with weapons funneled through Pensacola, Florida.

The result was a ferocious frontier war which raged across the West. During the summer of 1776, a Cherokee war chief named Dragging Canoe (Tsiyu-Gunsini) ravaged at least a dozen frontier settlements. In addition, the Iroquois of New York sided with the British under the leadership of the Mohawk chief Joseph Brant. Other Iroquois tribes joined Brant, however, the Oneidas and Tuscaroras decided to side with the Americans.

During the summer of 1778, Iroquois warriors, alongside Loyalist forces, raided settlements in New York. The Continental Army pursued them, in August of 1779, and destroyed dozens of Iroquois villages and thousands of acres of crops ready for harvest. This action pitted Iroquois against one another on the battlefield for the first time in over two centuries.

Much of the fighting on the frontier involving Americans, the British, and various native groups was brutal, savage, and chaotic. Indian activities included scalping, torture, and the killing of women and children. But such activities were not limited to the actions taken by Native Americans. Both American and British fighters engaged in such activities, as well, as they fought across the American frontier.

Review and Write

How did the American Revolution involve Native Americans?

The Frontier Revolution

Although most of the fighting of the American Revolution took place east of the Appalachians, at sites such as Brandywine, Pennsylvania, Monmouth Courthouse, New Jersey, and Camden, South Carolina, some of the bloodiest engagements were fought on the frontier in the Ohio Country. One of the most successful and, perhaps, notorious of the American leaders fighting in the West was George Rogers Clark, who, in 1777, was a 24-year-old frontier fighter who had developed a plan to take control of the Northwest Territory—the region of the modern-day states of Ohio, Indiana, and Illinois.

After meeting with the governor of Virginia, patriot leader Patrick Henry, Clark prepared to take his men west. His plan was to gather a force of frontiersmen, recruits from Ohio and northern Kentucky, march them down the Ohio River to capture the British outposts in the Illinois Country. These sites were strategic and established centers of frontier populations.

Clark's men were able to reach the British post at Kaskaskia and capture the fort without firing a shot. Many of the citizens of the outpost were French, since the British had acquired the post from France after the French and Indian War. They appeared surprised to discover that they and Clark's men were to be considered allies. (France had entered the American Revolution as an American ally the previous year.)

The Illinois settlement of Cahokia fell to Clark next—then the town of Vincennes, site of the British Fort Sackville. As Clark's men marched, they also fought Indians, subduing tribe after tribe. Although George Clark was not fond of Indians, he was able to negotiate with them, and, in some cases, form alliances.

As Clark rampaged throughout the Illinois Country, word of his exploits reached the British stationed at Fort Detroit. British Lieutenant Colonel Henry Hamilton intended to challenge Clark with a contingent of British regular troops, along with 500 Indian allies and some Loyalist forces. Hamilton was known in the West as "the Hair Buyer," since he had made a practice of buying hundreds of frontier scalps from loyal Indians. His march carried him to Vincennes where he recaptured Fort Sackville. When Clark heard of Hamilton's success, he returned to Vincennes with his forces. He and his men made a legendary march through the winter, suffering through icy waters and freezing temperatures, to surprise Hamilton at Vincennes. On occasion, to bolster the spirits of his men, Clark held war dances. Clark continued to push his forces, accepting nothing less than surprise and success against Hamilton.

When Clark arrived at Vincennes on February 23, 1779, he sent word to the French residents in the town that he had returned and intended to take back the fort. Clark's men were deadly shots and made regular practice of picking off the British soldiers inside the fort by firing through the small loopholes and cannon ports along the wooden walls of the fort.

Following a spirited engagement throughout a night of rifle and cannon fire, the British surrendered the fort by morning on the 24th. Not one of Clark's men had even been wounded during the night battle. When Clark took a group of Hamilton's Indian allies prisoner, he ordered them bound and executed by his own hand, since each carried white scalps on his belt. One by one, George Clark struck them with a tomahawk. With the fall of Vincennes again, Clark retained control of the Illinois Country for the remainder of the war. Yet, Clark was disappointed in his efforts in support of the patriot cause, since he never managed to bring about the fall of Detroit.

Review and Write

1. What plan did frontiersman George Rogers Clark present to the governor of Virginia concerning the occupation of the lands of the Ohio Country during the Revolutionary War?

2. What sort of problems did Clark and his men encounter in the western frontier?

The Post-Revolutionary Frontier

The American Revolution brought extraordinary change to the 13 colonies engaged in war against the British. The 13 original colonies became states, banding together to form the United States of America and thus declared their independence from Britain. The fighting dragged on for six-and-a-half years until 1781, when the British General Cornwallis surrendered to General Washington at the sleepy little tobacco port of Yorktown, Virginia. Another two years would pass, however, before the the Treaty of Paris was signed in 1783 ending the war. Under this treaty, the United States was ceded land from the Atlantic Ocean to the Mississippi River; from the Great Lakes to Spanish Florida.

Gone were the British officials, along with the Proclamation of 1763, which had officially closed the frontier to colonial migration. Now, it was to be the United States government that would determine future policies regarding the western frontier. Many Americans, especially those already living in the Trans-Appalachian region were understandably ecstatic.

The Indians of the West, however, were left dazed and friendless. The British abandoned them, having lost the war. Yet the Native Americans had never officially surrendered to the Americans and did not feel they had been defeated. But in the minds of the victors, they had beaten the allies of the British, as well. Even those Indians who had allied themselves with the patriots, such as the Oneidas, would be left to fend for themselves against encroaching Anglo-Americans.

Despite the Proclamation of 1763, and the Revolutionary War itself, western migration had never ceased. After an entire generation of westward movement, such remote places as Kentucky and Tennessee were home to thousands. By 1785, the non-Indian population of Kentucky (which remained technically part of the state of Virginia until receiving its own statehood in 1792) had mushroomed to more than 30,000. By the end of the decade, another 45,000 had joined them. In Tennessee, 36,000 immigrants had established their frontier homes. Getting late into the game,

immigration was picking up for the Ohio Country north of the Ohio River.

Despite the American success in its revolution, there were still problems to face involving European powers. The British did not immediately abandon their western forts, even though they had agreed to under the Treaty of Paris. (They would not completely give up those western outposts until 1796!) Spain, which controlled the vast lands of Louisiana, just west of the Mississippi River, would not accept American dominance east of the river and blocked American access to this vital trade route in the North American interior.

To many Americans, the key to future growth for the United States lay in the lands of the Trans-Appalachian West. Congress gave the region much attention, intending to secure the rights, privileges and loyalty of the independently minded pioneers who lived there.

When the Confederation Government of the United States sent its appointed secretary for foreign affairs, John Jay, to negotiate with the British and the Spanish over the above noted issues, he had little luck. Security in the western territories for the Americans living there appeared to remain an illusive dream.

But the American government, operating under the nation's first national constitution, the Articles of Confederation, did manage to organize its western territories politically. During the decade or so of its existence under the Articles, the U.S. government took up the problem of establishing its authority in the West.

Review and Write

1. What information on this page reveals how ineffective the Proclamation of 1763 was?

2. Following the Revolutionary War, the United States took possession of the lands west of the Appalachian Mountains. How had the region grown in its white population by the 1780s?

Organizing the Northwest Territory

The year was 1784. The American Revolution had just ended with the signing of the Treaty of Paris the previous year. With the Articles of Confederation, the Confederation Congress controlled the lands west of the Appalachians and intended to organize the western territories as quickly and as efficiently as possible. In relatively short order, the Congress passed a pair of laws related to the West, especially the Northwest Territory.

By definition, the western border of the United States at the end of the American Revolution was the Mississippi River. The region comprising the Northwest included the modern-day states of Ohio, Indiana, Illinois, Michigan, Wisconsin, and part of Minnesota. How government would be organized in those western territories was given extensive attention by Congress.

It was determined in 1784 that the western lands would be divided into states and that a western population would first experience territorial status, and eventually statehood.

In 1785, the Confederation Congress passed the Land Ordinance of 1785. This congressional act established the machinery for a federally-sponsored survey of the Old Northwest and for the sale of western lands. American leaders had learned from the mistakes made in land organization in Kentucky, where a chaotic combination of overlapping and sometimes inaccurate surveys created awkward land claims, many of which could never be legitimized.

To avoid a repeat of such land squabbles, the Confederation Congress called for the dividing of the land into square townships, measuring six miles by six miles. Each township was divided into 36 sections, each measuring one mile square. In each section the number of acres was 640. The land within each section of a township was to then be offered for sale to the public at a price equivalent to $1 per acre. Thus, a pioneer could buy 640 acres, a square mile of territory, for an equal number of dollars. (The amount per acre was equivalent to about $120 in 1990 dollars.)

The sections of each township were numbered as shown in the illustration. It was determined that the profits from the sale of Section 16 would be held in reserve for the support of local schools. In addition, Sections 8, 11, 26, and 29 were reserved for later sale.

The original survey in the Old Northwest was designated to begin in Ohio, along the banks of the Ohio River, at a point where the eastern border of Ohio, northern Virginia, and western Pennsylvania coincide. From that point, surveyors laid down a Geographer's Base Line to the Muskingum River. The first seven townships extending east-to-west were referred to as the Seven Ranges. This pattern of squares soon became the settlement pattern across the United States, continuing into the Great Plains and the Far West for the next century.

Another act passed by the Confederation Congress was the Northwest Ordinance of 1787. Under this act, Congress established a governmental system for the Old Northwest. The act allowed the eventual creation of no more then five and no fewer than three states to be carved out of the region. It also recognized the rights of Americans living there, making them identical to the rights enjoyed by citizens in the original 13 states. Slavery was prohibited in the region. In terms of governance, once the free white male residents of a territory reached 5000, they could establish a territorial assembly, but the territorial governor would have veto power over all legislation.

Such laws helped to organize and streamline western occupation of the Northwest Territory.

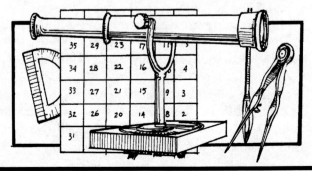

Indian Campaigns in Ohio

Although such frontier-related acts as the Land Ordinance of 1785, and the Northwest Ordinance of 1787, were among the few successful pieces of legislation passed by the Confederation Congress, they also created problems for Native Americans in the region. But the handwriting was already on the wall for the tribes of the northern Ohio Country.

Under two additional Indian treaties, the second Treaty of Fort Stanwix (1784) and the Treaty of Fort McIntosh (1785), the Iroquois and several Ohio tribes were forced to surrender ownership of part of their traditional lands in eastern Ohio. This was all done hastily and under duress, pushing the Native Americans out of the way so that the region could be surveyed and parceled out to willing frontiersmen.

Desperate for a national cash flow, the government, in short order, sold 1.5 million acres of this land. In fact, land sales outstripped the survey, and thousands of western migrants poured into Ohio and occupied land without clear title or purchase. In 1885, Congress ordered national troops into Ohio to remove the interlopers, but the squatters returned after the soldiers left. Despite its results, the Northwest Ordinance of 1787 did attempt to reestablish relations between the U.S. government and the Ohio Country Indians. Under the act, Congress recognized the independence of the Indian nations. Congressmen also attempted to further define U.S.-Indians relations on the frontier through an additional act, called the Indian Intercourse Act (1790). This act sought to protect natives from dishonest white traders. The act was a positive step toward smoothing out hostilities the western tribes were developing toward the new American government.

In addition, the Indian Intercourse Act addressed further the issue of Indian sovereignty and nationhood. The act specified that all future Indian land acquisitions made by the U.S. government would require the writing of a treaty made available to the public. On the surface, the act appeared to indicate the will of the government to negotiate with Native Americans in good faith in the future.

But the act was soon misused and abused. The government continued to apply military force against tribes who were unwilling to cede land to Anglo-Americans. Thus, a cycle of Indian land cessions continued. A raging bitterness continued to develop among Ohio tribes until they finally took military action of their own. By 1790, such tribes as the Shawnees, Delawares, and others united under Chief Little Turtle.

That fall, Little Turtle and his warriors fought a contingent of troops under the command of General Josiah Harmar in Ohio and defeated them badly. A year later, in November 1791, the same Indians crushed forces led by General Arthur St. Clair, the governor of the Northwest Territory, killing or wounding nearly 1000 men. The loss would stand as the worst defeat inflicted by Indians on an army in American history.

Such successes prompted the British in Canada to ally themselves in spirit with the Ohio Indians. The British built a new post, Fort Miami in northern Ohio, and met with Indians there.

St. Clair's defeat prompted President George Washington to dispatch a significant force of American troops into the Ohio frontier under the command of General Anthony Wayne. Known as "Mad Anthony," Wayne engaged the Indians in the battle of Fallen Timbers on August 20, 1794. The northern Ohio battle was a crushing blow to the Native Americans. When the defeated warriors attempted to take sanctuary among the British at Fort Miami, they found the gate of the frontier fortress closed to them.

Opening the Way West

"Mad Anthony" Wayne's victory at Fallen Timbers in the fall of 1794, was a destructive blow to the Ohio Country tribes. Under such a great loss, the warriors were forced to agree to a new land negotiation, called the Treaty of Greenville (1795). This treaty called for the Indians to cede the southern half of Ohio to the United States, plus a portion of Indiana. In addition, the Northwest Territory settlements of towns such as Detroit, as well as the newer, small settlement of Chicago on Lake Michigan, were also granted over to American control.

This treaty gave the American government a new footing in the frontier region. It solidified their strength and furthered their legitimacy in the West as a true nation with regional power. For the British, they understood that they would never reverse American presence in the Northwest Country. Through negotiations involving American diplomat John Jay, the British agreed to abandon the last of their old forts which they had never surrendered following the Treaty of Paris (1783). The year was 1794. Symbolically, Jay's Treaty was a great diplomatic victory for the young United States, which eliminated any significant presence by the British on American soil.

The next year, 1795, another American diplomat, Thomas Pinckney, began negotiations with the Spanish over the southern boundary of the United States. Up to that time, the Spanish had claimed portions of the Old Southwest (the modern-day states of Mississippi, Alabama and Tennessee). But a newly weakened Spain had just been defeated by the French in war, making it impossible for Spain to force their claims in America. Pinckney was able to write a treaty with the Spanish that recognized the 31st parallel as the boundary between the American Southwest and Spanish Florida. In addition, Pinckney's Treaty reopened the Spanish-controlled Mississippi River to American trade traffic once again. This agreement alone was great news for many of those Americans living in the Trans-Appalachian region. They needed to rely on access to the Mississippi River and the Spanish port of New Orleans for shipping their western produce to market.

Trans-Appalachian pioneer farmers, producing everything from corn to hemp, wheat to hogs, and cotton to whiskey, needed access to viable markets for their agricultural produce. Hauling their goods overland by freight wagon was especially prohibitive due to the high costs. Instead, thousands of western Americans each year would build flatboats, load them with baskets of corn, bushels of wheat, bales of cotton, jugs of whiskey or herds of hogs and float their wares down local rivers—the Tennessee, Cumberland, Wabash, and others—to the Ohio River, then continue down that lengthy stream to the Mississippi.

Ultimately these intrepid pioneer boatman would reach the port of New Orleans where they would sell their goods, accumulate much needed cash, then make their way back to their homes in Tennessee, Kentucky, or Ohio on horseback or on foot, traveling overland across a heavily forested trail called the Natchez Trace. Pinckney's Treaty was greatly lauded by westerners everywhere.

With both Jay's Treaty and Pinckney's Treaty in hand, the United States could finally take true possession of their western territories. The British threat, for the time being, was eliminated; Spain was on friendly terms; and the French were far removed from their former empire in North America. It appeared, as the end of the 18th century approached, that the United States would soon become the most powerful nation in all of North America.

Review and Write

1. How did Jay's Treaty and Pinckney's Treaty improve life on the American frontier?

2. What roles did Anthony Wayne, John Jay, and Thomas Pinckney play in providing security and economic vitality for pioneer farmers during the 1780s and 1790s?

The Russian Frontier

With the approaching new century, the United States was changing rapidly and so, also, the American frontier. The country's first constitution, the Articles of Confederation had proven too weak and ineffective, causing Americans to scrap the document, and with it the loose confederation of states, replacing it with a new Constitution. This new framework strengthened the national government dramatically. America gained a presidency with George Washington serving as the country's first Chief Executive. Even in his younger days, Washington had often focused on the West, working on survey parties, fighting the British in the wilderness, erecting forts, investing in a frontier canal project, and purchasing Western lands. By 1800, much of the nation's focus was on the Western frontier, as well.

America's population growth almost demanded that the country look west. Between 1790 and 1800, the American census rose from 3.9 million people to 5.3 million. And the traditional disincentives for moving onto the frontier were being eliminated. The Native American population in the Trans-Appalachian region numbered around 100,000 people, far too low a number to effectively challenge the constant stream of migrants headed west. The people living in what had been remote corners of Ohio, Kentucky, and Tennessee began witnessing the arrival of more and more neighbors, with the development of frontier communities, villages, and towns.

With the Spanish reopening the Mississippi River to western trade, pioneer farmers had a ready market for their farm produce.

While Americans in 1800 were intent on "the West" they owned, located east of the Mississippi River, there were other frontiers just as active and viable west of the Mississippi. Across the lands of the Far West, international frontiers occupied by Russian, Spanish, and French pioneers were flourishing. From California to Alaska to the vast expanses of Spanish- and French-occupied Louisiana, these early settlements, in what would one day be part of the United States, laid the framework for cultures and social systems, some of which have endured into the 21st century.

Throughout the 1700s, the Russians busied themselves in the lands now known as Alaska, establishing a frontier based on the fur trade. As early as 1741, the Russian czar, Peter the Great, had sent a Danish sea captain, Vitus Bering, on an expedition from Siberia, across the sea which was to be named for him, to the Aleutian Islands, as well as to the Alaskan mainland. While Bering died on the return trip, a victim of a shipwreck, news of the abundance of furs sparked others to follow in his footsteps.

By the 1750s, the Russians had established an extensive trading empire in Alaska, with furs as the chief commodity. However, the trade was not always friendly between the Russians and the Native American Inuits and Aleuts. War broke out repeatedly. In one encounter, in 1762, known as the Aleut Revolt, the Alaskan natives destroyed a fleet of Russian ships. After four years of fighting, the Aleuts were finally defeated.

Despite their clashes, longtime contact between Russian men and Aleut women produced a significant number of "Russian creoles," who often played significant roles in the Alaskan fur trade as traders, interpreters, company clerks, and explorers.

By 1784, Russian merchant, Gregory Shelikhov, established the first permanent Russian settlement in Alaska. By the turn of the century, the Russian-American Company had established a series of fur trading bases stretching from Alaska as far south as Fort Ross, just north of San Francisco Bay.

Review and Write

1. What was the result of warfare between the Aleuts and the Russians?

2. What efforts were involved for the Russians to establish themselves in the Pacific Northwest throughout the 1700s? Who was involved?

The Spanish West

While the Russians consolidated control of the fur trade in Alaska, establishing themselves as far south as northern California, other European powers were busy in the western half of modern-day United States, as well. One such power was Spain.

Imperial Spain had arrived in the New World at the end of the 1400s, and had spent over two and-a-half centuries establishing and fortifying a New World empire throughout the Caribbean, Mexico, Central America, and the American Southwest. By the 1770s, the Spanish had explored the entire coast of California, laying claim to the lands watered by the Columbia River (which forms much of the border between modern-day Oregon and Washington states). Spanish ships had also reached Vancouver Island and southeastern Alaska, putting them in the same American neighborhood as the Russians.

This same region was also home to British outposts, as British fur traders had built a trading fort on Vancouver Island's Nootka Sound in 1789. Even Americans were present there before the end of the 18th century, arriving in the region of the Pacific Northwest by ship in 1787. They were soon in control of the lucrative sea otter trade, however, but the Americans did not establish any significant settlements there.

Concerned about the movement of Russians into California waters, the Spanish attempted to bedrock their presence in the region. While their presence in northern California had always been limited, the Spanish began building a series of 21 Catholic missions from San Diego in the far south (1769) to Sonoma in the north (1823). The largest of these frontier mission outposts, where Catholic fathers attempted to convert local natives and establish extensive farming—including many vineyards and orchards—was Los Angeles. Situated along the southern California coast amid fertile valleys pampered by mild temperatures, the Los Angeles mission included a native population of 300 mestizos, those having both Spanish and Indian ancestors.

While Spain's influence in California expanded throughout the 1700s, other significant European outposts were also growing west of the Mississippi River. The French-influenced community of New Orleans, founded in 1718, by French explorer Jean Baptiste le Moyne, Sieur de Bienville, was becoming a thriving port city. Located at the mouth of the Mississippi River, it was the final destination of frontier Americans who shipped their western produce down American rivers.

Although founded as a French settlement, New Orleans, as well as the vast expanse of Louisiana, came into Spanish hands following the French and Indian War in 1763. But the original French influence in New Orleans remained ingrained in the culture of its people, primarily a mixture of whites and blacks. By 1800, New Orleans was home to 8000 citizens, half being white and the half being black. But others—Spanish, Americans, English, Germans, Irish, and the Creoles, a mixed people of French and Indian heritage—also lived in frontier New Orleans. By 1801, the city's port was shipping over $3 million in produce overseas.

Further north, 600 miles up the Mississippi River, another French settlement was establishing its frontier presence. Established in 1763 by French trader Pierre Laclede, the river settlement of St. Louis served as an outpost for the western fur trade located along the Missouri River to the west. St. Louis, in 1800, was home to 1000 residents. Not yet a significant western presence, St. Louis was destined to become one of the crossroads of the American frontier.

Part I.

Matching. *Match the answers shown below with the statements given above. Place the letters of the correct answers in the spaces below.*

1. Mohawk chief during the American Revolutionary War
2. Virginia governor who, in 1774, encouraged a war with the Shawnee to gain their land
3. Trans-Appalachian territory which became the 14th state in the Union in 1792
4. Authorized by President Washington to establish a trail across Ohio in 1796
5. Gravel-topped road established across Pennsylvania in 1790s
6. Name denoting the handle of an axe
7. A type of inexpensive metal produced by combining copper and tin; used by frontiersmen
8. Practice of removing a ring of bark from the base of a tree to cause it to die
9. Temporary, open-sided structure built by pioneer families
10. Cabin floor consisting of split logs laid down with the rounded half toward the ground
11. Cherokee war chief who destroyed a dozen frontier settlement during summer of 1776
12. Treaty under which the Cherokees ceded large tract of land on upper Tennessee River

A. Kentucky   B. poll   C. lean-to   D. Joseph Brant
E. Earl of Dunmore   F. Lancaster Pike   G. "girdling"   H. Dragging Canoe
I. Hard Labor   J. Ebenezer Zane   K. pewter   L. puncheon

1. ____ 2. ____ 3. ____ 4. ____ 5. ____ 6. ____ 7. ____ 8. ____ 9. ____ 10. ____ 11. ____ 12. ____

Part II.

Matching. *Match the answers shown below with the statements given above. Place the letters of the correct answers in the spaces below.*

1. American frontiersman during the Revolutionary War who captured Vincennes and Cahokia
2. Danish sea captain who sailed from Siberia to the Aleutian Islands in 1740s
3. British fort located in the Old Northwest frontier settlement of Vincennes
4. American diplomat who negotiated with British over evacuation of Old Northwest forts
5. Square grid used to survey western lands which comprised 36 square miles of territory
6. U.S. government act which attempted to protect natives from dishonest white traders
7. Delaware Indian chief who defeated General Harmar in Ohio in 1790
8. American general defeated by Native Americans in Ohio during November, 1791 battle
9. American general who defeated Native Americans in battle of Fallen Timbers in 1794
10. Name of treaty between United States and Spain which reopened Mississippi River
11. British officer known as the "Hair Buyer"
12. French founder of the community of New Orleans in 1718

A. Fort Sackville   B. Indian Intercourse   C. Anthony Wayne   D. Sieur de Bienville
E. Henry Hamilton   F. township   G. Arthur St. Clair   H. Vitus Bering
I. George Clark   J. John Jay   K. Little Turtle   L. Pinckney

1. ____ 2. ____ 3. ____ 4. ____ 5. ____ 6. ____ 7. ____ 8. ____ 9. ____ 10. ____ 11. ____ 12. ____

Frontier Cincinnati

It would remain for future generations of Americans to incorporate such western settlements as New Orleans, Los Angeles, and St. Louis into the American territorial landscape. In the meantime, Americans continued to push into the Trans-Appalachian region in greater numbers, with the arrival of the 19th century. As a result, American communities developed that were destined to become significant urban centers before the end of the 1800s.

By 1800, the number of pioneers living in the West, between the Appalachians and the Mississippi River had reached 500,000. Many of them had come originally from Virginia and North Carolina, in search of inexpensive, yet fertile farm land. They settled along the various western flowing rivers of the region, including the Tennessee, the Cumberland, and, of course, the Ohio. Already, two states had been carved out of the backwoods settlements: Kentucky (1792) and Tennessee (1796), making them the 14th and 15th states of the Union.

This movement of Americans knew no bounds during the years just prior to, and just after 1800. Americans were restless, seeking greater opportunities over the next horizon. For that reason, nearly one out of every 10 American families moved annually. Throughout the Atlantic Coast states, approximately one in three rural families had moved between the 1790 and 1800 censuses. Many such moves were simply lateral, involving a short distance between rural communities or towns. But many others moved greater distances, as much as hundreds of miles. To facilitate these migrations, the western settlers used the various rivers of the region to move their families, household truck, and livestock by flatboat to greener pastures.

Despite the rural nature of the western settlements, some communities of significance were established. One of the most important towns on the frontier, by 1800, was Cincinnati, Ohio. Situated 450 miles west of Pittsburgh,

Cincinnati was founded by Mathias Denman in 1788, as the settlement of Losantville. Within two years, Losantville was renamed Cincinnati, after the highly popular Revolutionary War veterans organization, the Society of the Cincinnati.

In its early years, Cincinnati was little more than a fort, intended to protect pioneers living along the Ohio and Miami Rivers. Indian attacks were common, and violence involving the Shawnee and Miami Native Americans caused the region to be known as "the Slaughterhouse."

But following the 1794 defeat of the Indians in the battle of Fallen Timbers, Cincinnati was on its way. The town developed, becoming a popular site of departure for frontier families headed down the Ohio River, bound for Indiana, Illinois, or Kentucky. At the turn of the century, Cincinnati was home to 750 people; ten years later, nearly 2500 people lived there.

In time, Cincinnati became more than an important river town on the American frontier. It developed as a major western meatpacking center, with facilities for the slaughter of hogs causing the town be referred to as "Porkopolis." Other industries, including the manufacture of soap, shoes, boots, and candles all derived from animal by-products, were thriving in the diversified economy of frontier Cincinnati.

The growth of such western cities could not be ignored with the passage of each decade of the 1800s. While no cities west of the Appalachians were among the top ten in population even as late as 1820 (except for French New Orleans), by 1850, the top ten list included Cincinnati, New Orleans, St. Louis, Pittsburgh, and Louisville in Kentucky.

Review and Write

1. How did Cincinnati progress from a frontier outpost to a thriving business community?

2. How did the battle of Fallen Timbers alter the history of the frontier outpost called Cincinnati?

The National Road

As the number of Americans moving into the Trans-Appalachian region increased after 1800, the primary route into the western interior of Ohio, Indiana, Kentucky, or Illinois was the Ohio River. This natural waterway provided a suitable transportation route free to all pioneers. But the demand for better roads into the western region brought about the passage of an act in the U.S. Congress in 1802. Not only did the act provide for Ohio statehood, but it also authorized the construction of an east-west road. This land route would come to be known as the National or Cumberland Road. By 1806, the federal government decided to extend the road from the Atlantic Ocean to the Mississippi River.

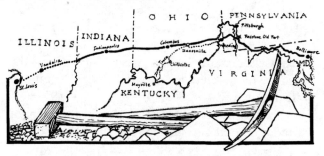

No extensive construction on this important artery west began until 1808. Road building was a slow, laborious process. The route began in Maryland and did not even reach the Ohio border, near the settlement of Wheeling, until 1818. The section running between Baltimore and Cumberland had been completed in 1814.

Nearly a generation passed before even the survey work for the road was begun in the Trans-Appalachian region of Ohio, Indiana, and Illinois. And construction did not begin in those territories or states until 1825. The road finally reached Columbus, Ohio, in 1833; was extended to Indiana by 1837; and hit the Illinois border in 1850. To that point, the National Road was a paved thoroughfare. Across Illinois, to St. Louis, the road continued, unpaved.

The pace of the construction of the National Road was determined, in part, by the amount of planning and work involved. The driving surface of the road was 30 feet wide, much wider than nearly any other road in America at that time. This width was intended to accommodate the passing of two wagons, including stagecoaches. The road was a gravel-top route, paved with an inch of crushed stone, and a layer of gravel laid on top of it. Usually, the surveyors attempted to lay the route along level ground, to help eliminate the need for grading, since such work was time consuming and costly.

Although the National Road was intended as the ultimate in land route construction, some of the techniques used appear extraordinary today. Trees were cleared from the route, but oddly enough, the stumps might be left behind. Trees measuring 18 inches or less in circumference were cut down, leaving 9-inch-high stumps. Trees measuring greater than 18 inches, were cut 15 inches from the ground. Such stumps proved a hazard for traffic on the route. The builders included pull-offs along the route, built on both sides of the frontier highway. These side strips measured 25 feet in width and were intended to provide a place for wagon repairs, resting, or overnight camping.

When completed, the National Road represented a $7 million construction project, making it one of the most expensive transportation systems of its day. The road became a popular route into the western interior through 1850. Traffic flowed both east and west on the road, as pioneer families traveled west in increasing numbers, and farmers and western traders hauled their goods to eastern markets.

While there were many different types of traffic on the National Road, three types were common—Conestoga wagons, stagecoaches, and packhorse or mule trains. By modern standards, traffic moved slowly on the National Road, as on every frontier land route of the period. Even stagecoaches, the fastest vehicle on wheels in early 18th-century America, only averaged 5 or 6 miles an hour. Even at high speed, the early stagecoaches achieved speeds of only 10 or 12 miles an hour!

River Highways West

While land routes into the Trans-Appalachian West, including the Wilderness Trail, Forbes's Road, the Lancaster Pike, and, later, the National Road helped facilitate the movement of Americans, the rivers of the region, such as the Ohio River, provided key transportation links through the region. Traffic on these western rivers throughout the 1790s and for the next 30 or 40 years became commonplace. As pioneer farmers raised their crops and livestock, they used the rivers to deliver their goods to markets such New Orleans.

Two of the most common types of western rivercraft used prior to the development of the steamboat were flatboats and keelboats. Of the two, keelboats were piloted by professional crews who carried goods along western rivers for a fee. Such boats featured a keel, were generally 60 to 70 feet long and included a housing in the center of the craft. Keelboats sported a sail so they could move upriver and a crew which used long poles to "push" the boat upriver when the wind failed.

By comparison, flatboats were temporary boats used by farmers and others. First used on the Ohio River, they were easily constructed and featured a flat bottom to allow the boat to float safely in just a few feet of water. Such boats were generally nothing more than large, floating, wooden boxes. Usually rectangular in shape, the sides of the flatboat stood about five feet high. The overall dimensions of the boats differed depending on how they were to be used, sometimes ranging in size from 20 to 100 feet in length and from 10 to 25 feet wide. Hammered together out of rough hardwoods, the sides of most flatboats could stop a bullet fired from shore. Such fears were focused less on the potential for Indian attack than on the possibilities of attack by river pirates.

Most flatboats were on the smaller side, measuring about 12 or 14 feet wide and about 50 feet in length. Flatboats on the Ohio needed to be this size since the river narrowed at the Louisville site to a width of about 15 feet, creating the Falls of the Ohio, which were actually a series of rapids.

Since the flatboats had no means of propulsion, they were meant to float down-stream only. Maneuvering such an awkward craft was done with three long sweeps, or large paddles, sometimes called broadhorns. One sweep was located at the rear, or stern, of the boat. The other two were placed on either side. Sometimes a fourth sweep was included, placed at the bow, or front, of the boat. Called a gouger, this sweep helped give the craft better stability and helped steer the lumbering raft downriver.

Flatboats were generally open to the elements. Some included a small cabin in the center of the craft, where the crew could sleep. Cargo was stored about the open deck of the typical flatboat. Since flatboats were used to carry farm produce to market, these boats were floating warehouses burdened with crates, barrels, bales, and jugs. As many as 500 barrels or crates could be jammed onto the flatboat's deck. Cargoes might include fruits, vegetables, cotton, grain, sorghum, whiskey, and even livestock, including cattle, hogs, or chickens. Slaves, too, might be shipped by flatboat.

A trip on a flatboat down the Ohio River to New Orleans was often slow. An average crew of five members worked the sweeps, looked out for snags and sunken tree trunks in the water, and kept a sharp eye out for pirates. The 2,000-mile voyage from Pittsburgh to New Orleans took about six weeks, with the boat traveling 24 hours a day. By the 1840s, thousands of flatboats were in use on the Trans-Appalachian rivers and the Mississippi River.

Western Rivercraft

While flatboats and keelboats were commonly used on the western rivers, a variety of additional boat types were also used to carry passengers and freight into the Trans-Appalachian West and beyond. Specially designed for specific tasks, some of these boats were named for the rivers on which they were used. Among the types of specialized boats were pirogues, batteaus, mackinaws, Durham boats, and arks.

A pirogue was basically a large canoe. It measured about 50 feet in length and had a width of about eight feet. This boat could carry an entire pioneer family and their household truck, or goods. A bateau (sometimes spelled bateaux) was a large skiff. A skiff is a wide boat with a flat bottom constructed out of planking. Skiffs are typically tied to larger boats and used to tow the boat's crew to shore without having to dock the large craft. Like the pirogue, the bateau could carry a pioneer family and their goods. A pair of sweeps, or broadhorns, were used to steer the bateau. Such crafts could be poled back upriver.

A boat called a mackinaw was often used on the Far Western rivers, such as the Missouri. Commonly used by fur trappers and western traders, the mackinaw was 60 feet long and about 15 feet wide, with pointed or rounded sides. The boat was built on a raft of logs and featured vertical sides. Such crafts were typically used to carry a season's worth of fur pelts downriver to sites such as St. Louis.

A Durham boat was a form of keelboat shaped similarly to a birchbark canoe. Named for Robert Durham of Pennsylvania, they were in use as early as 1750, on eastern rivers, including the Delaware. Other Eastern keelboats included the Mohawk or Schenectady boats which were used on both those rivers respectively.

A popular form of flatboat in the Trans-Appalachian region was the ark. Originally used on Eastern rivers such as the Susquehanna and Delaware, it came to be used on western rivers, including the Ohio and the Mississippi. These large flatboats were 75 to 100 feet long and between 15 and 20 feet wide. Constructed out of heavy timbers and lumber planking, arks typically featured a large housing, giving them a similar appearance to a modern houseboat. A pioneer family might live on such an ark until they found suitable land.

The Ohio packet boat was a form of western keelboat which included a passenger cabin. The typical Ohio packet had the same dimensions as a standard ark. These boats included a mast and sails and could be maneuvered by a group of polers. Before the development of the steamboat, Ohio packets delivered passengers and freight between Pittsburgh and Louisville.

During the same years such boats were in use on America's rivers, some American inventors were busying themselves developing steam-powered crafts. Such a boat was powered by a steam engine and a paddle wheel. Called steamboats, they reinvented river travel in the 19th century.

Probably the most famous American steamboat inventor was Robert Fulton, who built and tested his steam-powered boat, the *Clermont*, in 1807, on the Hudson River. This unique and sleek craft was 150 feet long and 13 feet wide. It drew about two feet of water and had two paddle wheels, built on the boat's sides. On its first river trip, Fulton's boat traveled upstream 110 miles in 24 hours!

Within four years of Fulton's successful invention, a steamboat called New Orleans, was in use on the Ohio and Mississippi Rivers. Steamboats would change the nature of American river traffic during the 1800s.

Building the Erie Canal

Americans were always looking for new routes into the interior of the Trans-Appalachian region during the early decades of the 19th century. The federal government built roads such as the National Road. Even more importantly, states funded the construction of toll roads, canals, and railroads to facilitate the movement into their regions. In the 1820s alone, states spent $26 million on internal improvements. Just two states spent half that figure: New York and Pennsylvania.

One of the most unique transportation projects of this period took place in New York: the Erie Canal. Built between 1817 and 1825, the Erie Canal was more than 10 times longer than any previously constructed canal in America. The story of its construction is a tale of engineering wonder.

By definition, canals are man-made waterways which provide water transportation where none previously existed. While the American landscape is blessed with an abundance of lakes and rivers, sometimes these waterways served as impediments to western travel, blocking routes and slowing down migrants. A canal was sometimes built to connect existing natural waterways, resulting in a longer, unbroken transportation system. Such was the case with the Erie Canal.

The father of this canal was a New York politician, Governor DeWitt Clinton. His dream was of a canal linking New York City with the Great Lakes. But his plan was a daunting one. The canal would connect the Hudson and Mohawk Rivers to Lake Erie by covering the 364-mile distance between Albany and Buffalo, New York. Clinton's ambitions were so grand that his scheme was derided as "Clinton's Folly."

But when Clinton convinced the New York legislature to approve the bonds for construction and convinced enough backers to put up the funds for the project, Clinton's Folly was one step closer to reality. It was estimated the canal project would cost $7 million, a hefty sum in those days.

The engineering required for the Erie Canal was highly sophisticated. The canal was to be 40 feet wide, four feet deep, and 364 miles in length.

Three hundred bridges would also need to be built so people on either side of the canal could cross over it. Since the landscape rises 555 feet across central New York, formed by the northern ends of the Appalachians, the canal would require the construction of 83 locks, special water chambers designed to raise and lower boats passing along the full length of the canal. Twenty-seven of those locks were constructed in the 15 miles between Albany and Schenectady. In addition, the work would involve removing thousands of tree stumps and blasting rock out of the canal's path.

The work on the canal required thousands of workers, many recent immigrants from Ireland, working for 50 cents a day. (Back in Ireland, these same workers might be lucky to receive 10 cents daily.) To remove the many stumps, a special stump removing machine was invented by some ingenious canal workers. Rock barriers were removed by an explosive called Dupont's Blasting Powder, since dynamite and nitroglycerin had not yet been invented. A local substance, called trass, was used to cement the canal walls watertight.

When completed the Erie Canal served as an inspiration to future canal builders. The 1830s witnessed a canal-building craze in America. And no wonder: Prior to the canal, a farmer might pay $100 to send a ton of produce from Buffalo to New York City, with the trip requiring three weeks. On the Erie, that same ton could be shipped for $10 in about one week. By 1840, there were over 4000 miles of canals operating in the U.S.

Review and Write

1. Why was the Erie Canal such an expensive building project?

2. The Erie Canal proved a vital transportation link between the East and the early 19th century frontier. How did the canal fit into a pattern of internal improvements being undertaken at the time?

West by Steamboat

The Erie Canal was an immediate success even before it was completed in 1825. This man-made waterway provided cheap transportation of immigrants into the western frontier of the Old Northwest and beyond. By 1830, 50,000 people were traveling on the Erie Canal, bound for settlements in Ohio, Indians, and Illinois, and even west of the Mississippi River.

Either new towns sprang up along the Erie Canal, or older communities received a shot in the arm from the economics created by the waterway. Buffalo, Utica, and Rochester developed into key cities along the New York route. In its first decade of operation, the Erie Canal collected nearly $10 million in tolls, more than the entire cost of the building project itself. States jealously watched and hurriedly moved into the canal-building business. Between 1820 and 1840, over $200 million was spent on canals, and the majority of that sum was raised and spent by the states themselves. New canals connected destinations within Massachusetts; linked Philadelphia to Pittsburgh; and dotted the landscapes of frontier sites from Ohio to Illinois.

But even as America rallied behind canals as a profitable means of transportation, a new water-based transport system was developing. New Yorker Robert Fulton, inventor of a practical steamboat in 1807, had made possible the transformation of America's great river system. Steamboats, with their special power and well-oiled engines, were turning rivers into two-way streets. With this new invention, men and women could travel upstream against a river's current just as quickly and efficiently as they could travel downstream. Fulton's *Clermont* had been built as a Hudson River steamer, but it took only a few short years for steamboats to make their way further into the frontier.

After the successful run of an Ohio steamboat, built in 1811 by an inventor named Nicholas Roosevelt (an early relative of both Presidents Theodore and Franklin Roosevelt), to New Orleans and back again, the West witnessed the development of the steamboat craze in American history. By 1817, 14 steamboats plied their way up and down the Ohio and Mississippi Rivers. Two years later, the number had risen to over 60. Often, they were christened with exciting names such as *Vesuvius*, *Aetna*, *Independence*, *General Jackson*, and the *Zebulon M. Pike*.

In just a few short years, steamboats were also making their way up the Missouri River toward the Far West. In 1819, the steamboat *Independence* arrived at the Missouri River settlement of Franklin, Missouri. One of those watching the *Independence* steam up the river was a ten-year-old boy named Kit Carson, who grew up to become a famous frontier guide and explorer. By 1860, a steamboat completed a trip of the Missouri River, landing at Fort Benton, Montana, a site 2,200 miles upriver.

The arrival of the steamboat on the frontier changed the history of the Trans-Mississippi West. New Orleans soon became the most important port in America. In 1801, the value of the goods passing through New Orleans was about $4 million. By 1850, the value had risen to almost $100 million. Through the 1840s, New Orleans handled twice the amount of goods that shipped through the port of New York City.

Without question, the 1840s was the golden age of steamboating. These great river vessels, their dual smokestacks belching black smoke, were the standard for shipping, passenger service, and mail delivery—at least until the arrival of a new transportation innovation: the railroad.

Review and Write

1. How did the movement of steamboats into the West change the history of the Trans-Mississippi region?

2. Once the Erie Canal was completed in 1825, the man-made water system began having a dramatic impact on the frontier. What were some of these important changes?

Early Railroads

Perhaps no other transportation innovation continues to spark the imagination of Americans today than does the railroad. Closing in on a 200-year-old history, the railroad would become synonymous with the popular stereotype of the West: The great steam locomotive, its huge iron smokestack sending an eruption of black soot into the western sky; its brass steam whistle shrilly splitting the air as it pulls into a western train station, lined with anxious frontiersmen eager for a letter from back home or news from "up the track." It is a potent image which has endured into the modern era through countless western films and television programs.

But the earliest days of railroading in America were much quieter and less grand. One of the first working railroads in the United States was constructed in 1828, and funded by the city fathers of Baltimore, Maryland. Called the Baltimore and Ohio Railroad (B&O), the line was opened two years later, and consisted of 13 miles of track. By 1842, it had been extended to Cumberland, Maryland. Fourteen years later, the B&O had arrived in St. Louis.

Early rail locomotives were little more than underpowered steam engines mounted on a railcar with wheels. Such engines could achieve speeds of between five and ten miles an hour. In addition, the primitive steam technology made such early railroad efforts dangerous. Train car axles broke, steam boilers exploded, killing engineers and passengers alike. The first rails were wooden, not iron, and were strapped down to crossties, instead of being spiked into place as was later done. When a strap broke, the wooden tie sprang up, forming what railroaders called a snakehead. Such loose rails could tear through the bottom of a rail car and cause a serious accident.

But in time, railroad technology advanced, creating more powerful rail locomotives able to travel faster and pull longer trains of cars. During the 1830s, one of the key locomotive designers was Matthias William Baldwin. A jeweler by trade,

Baldwin became interested in railroads from their earliest models. One of his first locomotives, constructed in just six months, was called Old Ironsides. This engine could reach a speed of 28 miles an hour while pulling 30 tons. The six-ton Old Ironsides can be seen today in the Franklin Institute Museum in Philadelphia. Throughout a 30-year career in railroading, Baldwin perfected the steam locomotive. By his death in 1866, his company, the Baldwin Locomotive Works, had made and sold more than 1500 locomotives.

By 1837, 200 American railroads had either been built or were on the drawing boards. Earlier successful lines, such as the B&O, the Camden and Amboy, and the Charleston and Hamburg, had sparked interest in steam-powered trains. In 1851, one of the greatest of the Trans-Appalachian railroads, the Illinois Central, was chartered, taking rails to the Mississippi River. The IC would lay 700 miles of track in six years, and would connect lines running from Wisconsin through Illinois, to Cairo, where the Mississippi and Ohio rivers join. One of the branch lines of the IC had a terminus located at the frontier town of Chicago. The arrival of the railroad in Chicago caused the town to develop quickly, making it one of the largest in the Midwest today.

More and more railroads were built until, by 1861, the year the Civil War erupted, the total rail system in America was over 31,000 miles of track. Trains were making regular runs as far west as Iowa, Missouri, and even Texas.

The Louisiana Purchase

Shortly after the turn of the 18th century, the United States experienced a unique opportunity in purchasing real estate. Few Americans had given much thought about the lands owned by the Spanish, lying west of the Mississippi. They were intent, instead, in settling the Trans-Appalachian region, the Prairie Plains, and the Old Southwest. But through a stroke of luck, much of the territory to the Far West, the land called Louisiana, would come under American control by 1803.

When Jefferson became president, the western border of the United States was the Mississippi River. But as early as his first month in office, Jefferson received word from the U.S. minister to England, Rufus King, that the Spanish, who owned Louisiana, intended to cede part of that vast western territory to the French. Jefferson knew he would have more to fear from the French than he ever would the Spanish. But there was little he could do.

By late 1801, King sent Jefferson, through Secretary of State James Madison, a copy of the treaty authorizing the cession of Louisiana to the French. But the treaty was unclear exactly what land was included. Jefferson's main concern was the possible closing of the port of New Orleans to American trade. Also, he wanted Americans to have access to western Florida as a possible access route to New Orleans. Jefferson encouraged Robert Livingston, new U.S. foreign minister to France, to persuade France to transfer ownership of western Florida to the United States. But the French leader, Napoleon Bonaparte, refused to offer the Americans any concessions.

Napoleon's plan was to establish a New World empire for France once again. The French had been out of North America since the end of the French and Indian War nearly 60 years earlier. But, by 1802, Napoleon's scheme soon collapsed. Thousands of troops he dispatched to his newly acquired Louisiana were annihilated during a slave revolt on the French-controlled island of Santo Domingo. Thus, the official transfer of Louisiana from Spanish to French control did not take place.

However, Jefferson's fears did come true when the Spanish closed the port of New Orleans to American traffic in October 1802.

Jefferson attempted to move quickly. He dispatched James Monroe to France to join Livingston in offering to buy New Orleans and western Florida for $10 million. (Congress, in fact, had only authorized about $2 million.) When Monroe arrived, he and Livingston were surprised to find the French not only agreeable to the suggestion of America acquiring control of New Orleans and West Florida, but they were willing to offer the entire region of Louisiana to the Americans—for a price.

When the French ministers set the figure at $15 million, both Monroe and Livingston were unsure how to proceed. Not only were they not authorized to spend that amount, they had no instructions to purchase the whole of Louisiana. However, not to pass up the offer, the two envoys agreed to the French terms, signing a treaty dated April 30, 1803.

When the document reached Jefferson on July 14, 1803, Jefferson himself was unsure of how to respond. The Constitution did not authorize the acquisition of land, but Jefferson convinced himself of its appropriateness, noting he had the power to make treaties with foreign powers. By October, 1803, Congress ratified the treaty which added over 825,000 square miles of territory to the United States. The Louisiana Purchase increased America's economic resources, and created a new western frontier under U.S. control. Eventually, all or parts of 15 states were carved out of this land.

The Corps of Discovery

Even before the purchase of Louisiana, President Jefferson was intent on sending explorers into the western region. In time, that expedition would become the famous Lewis and Clark Expedition. The author of the Expedition was President Thomas Jefferson [1801–1809]. He had first thought of such an undertaking about the time the United States had achieved its independence, in 1783. On January 18, 1803, Jefferson asked Congress for authorization and an appropriation of $2500 to send a military expedition to explore the Missouri River to find its source in the Rocky Mountains, then to follow the western-flowing streams to the Pacific.

Jefferson gave two purposes for the proposed mission: to prepare the way for the expansion of the American fur trade to the tribes throughout the area to be explored; and to advance geographical knowledge of the continent. (At that time, the region was not yet owned by the United States.)

While the proposal was before Congress, events lined up in Jefferson's favor. By April 1803, the French had negotiated for the sale of the vast Louisiana Territory to the Americans. With that purchase, there were no realistic impediments to Congress authorizing such an expedition into the West.

To command the expedition, Jefferson chose his private secretary, Captain Meriwether Lewis of the First U. S. Infantry Regiment. With the president's approval, Lewis invited his old friend, William Clark, to be his co-leader. The two men had become friends while serving together in the army in the 1790s. Clark, younger brother of George Rogers Clark, the Revolutionary War hero of the West, quickly accepted.

For months prior to the start of the expedition, Lewis selected equipment to outfit the Corps of Discovery. He went to the federal arsenal at Harper's Ferry, Virginia, to choose weapons. He liked the Kentucky Long Rifle because it was a very accurate weapon at long-distance shooting. But he also redesigned the gun so that it would be stronger and last through the entire journey across the West. In addition, Lewis selected some small swivel cannon to mount on the crew's boats, as well as a new weapon called an air rifle.

To prepare him for his work as a leader of the expedition, Lewis studied and acquired new skills, including how to navigate by the stars. He studied under some of the leading scholars of the day, becoming familiar with such subjects as natural history, anatomy, and medicine. Lewis collected medicines for his party, including some strong laxative pills called Dr. Rush's Thunderbolts. In addition, he amassed scientific devices such as a microscope, hydrometers, sextant, and equipment for reading weather information.

Since establishing friendly Indian relations was a key part of the expedition's mission, Lewis collected a variety of gifts for the Native Americans he would encounter. The items included colored beads, mirrors, bells, metal cooking kettles, handkerchiefs, thimbles and needles, all colors of ribbons, and calico shirts. Lewis also took brass finger rings and dozens of peace medals to hand out to chiefs. These specially made medallions featured a picture of President Jefferson on one side and on the other, two hands clasped in friendship.

After making initial preparations in the East and receiving final and detailed instructions from the president, Lewis set out for the West on July 5, 1803, from Pittsburgh. Following the Ohio River, Lewis traveled by keelboat, picking up Clark and several recruits at Louisville, Kentucky. The group continued down the Ohio to the Mississippi River. They then went upriver to Wood River, Illinois, cross from the mouth of the Missouri River.

Review and Write

As President Thomas Jefferson dispatched the Lewis and Clark expedition west, he delineated specific objectives for the Corps of Discovery. What were those objectives.

Taking the Expedition West

Together Lewis and Clark worked hard putting their group of explorers together. When looking for volunteers for the mission, they carefully avoided men who wanted to go on the trip just for the adventure. Instead, they sought strong men who had worked on the frontier wilderness. Only men who were hard workers could be used on the long trip west.

Among the men selected for membership in the Corps of Discovery were skilled hunters, rivermen, blacksmiths, carpenters, and soldiers. Lewis and Clark both knew that their crew would need to supply meat for the exploring party, build boats for river travel, fix broken rifles, and construct log shelters and forts.

In the end, Lewis and Clark put together a group of 30 men including 17 soldiers, 11 enlistees, a half-Osage Indian interpreter named George Drouilliard, to help the men talk to the western Indians, and Clark's black man-servant named York. Most of the men were in their 20s, eager to participate—nearly all were unmarried. They also agreed to take along Lewis's pet dog, a Newfoundland named Scammon.

Besides these recruits, six soldiers—a corporal and five privates—plus several French boatmen were hired to travel with the expedition during the first year of the trip and then bring back down the Missouri River any new plants and animal specimens the group discovered and collected, as well as scientific information, including soil samples, weather information, and geological knowledge. In some ways, the Lewis and Clark expedition was to be a scientific study of the West which was still a mystery to many Americans, including those men ready to meet the challenges of a land unknown to them.

Through the winter of 1803-04, the Lewis and Clark party remained encamped at Wood River. During that time, the co-captains trained their men, collected additional equipment, and discussed what lay ahead with traders and boatmen who had previously been up the Missouri River some distance.

At the same time, Louisiana Territory was officially being turned over to the American government by the Spanish. With that exchange of authority, the Corps of Discovery was set to head up the Missouri by April 1804. For the next 28 months, the explorers would travel to the western edge of American territory and beyond. They would progress by river, on horseback, and on foot.

All the supplies were stored on a large keelboat and two pirogues, smaller flat-bottomed boats which could hold about ten men. On the afternoon of May 14, 1804, at four o'clock, the group of 45 men set sail up the Missouri. It was raining when they began their historic journey.

Traveling up the Missouri proved to be difficult. While the boats sailed when possible, the men also had to row against the current. When the boats reached rapids, the men went ashore and pulled the boats upstream with ropes. By mid-June, the crew settled into a routine which included anticipating rapids along the Missouri.

They made contact with Indians fairly early on. The Osage Indians along the river were friendly and traded deer meat for whiskey. The party pushed on, passing the place where Kansas City is located today, where the Kansas and Missouri rivers come together. The great Kansas prairies lay to the west. Here, the crew celebrated the Fourth of July, 1804, near modern-day Atchison, Kansas. The men fired guns for the holiday and danced to fiddle music played by one of the French boatmen. Everyone knew they should expect greater adventures ahead, as well as additional hardships.

Review and Write

1. What type of information did the Corps of Discovery record on their way up the Missouri River?

2. Describe some of the men who participated in the Corps of Discovery. How might you describe a "typical" member of the expedition?

Ascending the Missouri River

Throughout the summer and fall of 1804, the Corps of Discovery made its way up the Missouri River through lands which today comprise the western states of Missouri, Kansas, Nebraska, Iowa, and the Dakotas. Along the way, Lewis and Clark, as well as others, recorded scientific information. They kept journals and diaries of what they saw. They drew pictures of new and interesting plant life and animals they had never seen before.

Sometimes the going was rough. In mid-July, a great storm nearly destroyed the keelboat. A squall of high winds, with thunder and lightening, battered the men as they fought to keep the boat from crashing onto rocks.

A week later, the party reached the mouth of the Platte River. Here the men began to see signs of Indians: abandoned lodges and burial mounds. About 20 miles north of the present-day town of Council Bluffs (across the river from Omaha, Nebraska), Lewis and Clark sat down with Plains Indians tribes, including the Ottoes and the Missouri. The meeting went well, and Lewis and Clark gave the Indians an American flag, gunpowder, whiskey, various trinkets, and a specially tailored coat for one of the chiefs. Lewis explained to the Indians that they were now under a new leader, the Great White Father, President Jefferson. He also told them that they would have to begin trading with the Americans.

During these same days, one man in the Corps became ill. On August 19, Sergeant Charles Floyd lay in pain and neither Lewis or Clark knew what to do. The next day Floyd died, probably from appendicitis. Floyd's death would be the only mortal casualty of the entire expedition.

Not long after Floyd's passing, Lewis experienced his own brush with death. Jefferson had asked Lewis to examine the geology and minerals the expedition discovered. Lewis did geological work himself, finding alum, pyrites, copper, and cobalt. As part of his testing, Lewis would taste the ores. As a result of his testing for cobalt, he poisoned himself with arsenic. Only a purge of salts cured him.

During this leg of their western journey, the expedition ate well. There was plenty of game to hunt. On the northern prairies the group killed their first antelope and shot many different kinds of birds. They captured a pelican. For science sake, they filled the bird's beak with water to see how much it would hold (five gallons). The men also saw a new creature on the plains—a burrowing animal which stood on its hind legs, yapping at the party—a prairie dog. Some of the men spent several hours trying to catch one of these elusive creatures. After great effort, they succeeded and sent the animal's skin and skeleton back to President Jefferson.

By the end of October 1804, the exploring party found themselves in what is today North Dakota. They made friends with the Mandan and Minnetaree Indians along the Knife River. Here Lewis and Clark agreed to make winter camp, knowing the Missouri River would soon begin freezing over, restricting their travel.

Here the men built a log fort which they called Fort Mandan. The buildings were completed by Christmas Day when Lewis and Clark raised the U.S. flag. During the winter months, the expedition's leaders talked to Indians and French Canadians in the village about what they should expect upriver come spring. One of these Canadians, a trapper-trader named Toussaint Charbonneau, agreed to take the expedition upriver.

But Lewis and Clark were more interested in Charbonneau's wife, a 15-year-old Shoshone woman named Sacajawea, who came from the lands to the west.

—"One of the Fairest Portions of the Globe"—

Sacajawea had been captured by the Minnetarees five years earlier when she was only ten or eleven years old. As a Shoshone, she would be able to serve as a guide and interpreter for Lewis and Clark, for her people lived to the west, near the Rocky Mountains.

By November 1804, the Missouri River began to freeze and the snows began to accumulate. The Mandans invited the white men to join them for the final buffalo hunt of the year. Half the expedition went on the hunt and killed ten buffalo.

As the winter grew colder, Lewis recorded temperatures as low as 40 degrees below zero. The men stayed busy hunting and gathering firewood. During one February hunting trip, Clark led more than half the expedition's men 20 miles down the frozen Missouri for a week. During that time, they killed 40 deer, three buffalo, and 16 elk. This produced 3,000 pounds of meat, but much of it was stolen by a band of Teton Sioux, numbering close to 100 warriors.

Other tribes of Indians visited the Mandans, looking for shelter, since the Mandans lived in round earth-mounds, which stayed warm during the cold winter months. Among those Indians who arrived were the Gros Ventres, a western tribe. They told Lewis and Clark that they would have to cross high mountains on horseback to get to the Columbia River, which flowed to the Pacific Coast. The captains knew they would have to buy horses from the Shoshone. Having Sacajawea with them would be extremely important, indeed. But she had her own problems, having given birth to a son in the dead of winter.

As the season turned to spring, the Corps of Discovery built six canoes, knowing their keelboat would not take them beyond the upper reaches of the Missouri River. By the end of March, the river's ice began to thaw and the men returned to buffalo hunting, adding to their supply of dried meat.

During the first week of April 1805, Lewis and Clark were ready to push on. Those men under one-year contracts loaded the keelboat with the party's scientific specimens and caged animals. The packing list included the bones of a coyote and pronghorn sheep, buffalo robes, a Mandan bow with a quiver of arrows, exotic plants, and a yapping prairie dog.

On April 7, 1805, at 4 A.M., the Corps of Discovery set out up the Missouri River. The main party now consisted of 31 men, Sacajawea and her two-month-old son, Pompey. As they left the Mandan camp, the Frenchmen and others headed south, back to St. Louis. Few of the men in both groups would ever see the others again. And for the men with Lewis and Clark, their trip would take them into a great unknown.

More adventures lay ahead for the Lewis and Clark expedition. Grizzly bears became a serious problem. A few weeks out from Fort Mandan, Lewis shot a buffalo. Before he had time to reload, a grizzly attacked him. Lewis ran into the river to get away from the huge beast. On another occasion, Clark and another man went ashore after spotting two grizzlies. One of the bears attacked the men. Between them, they shot the bear ten times before it collapsed and then only after it swam half-way across the Missouri. Although killing grizzlies was dangerous work, the men found the meat very tasty, and a large bear could be rendered to make five to eight gallons of cooking fat.

The Corps passed into Montana, witnessing some of the most exotic scenery of the expedition. As the party continued, Lewis wrote of what he saw: "This immense river waters one of the fairest portions of the globe. Nor do I believe that there is in the universe a similar extent of country. As we passed on, it seemed those scenes of visionary enchantment would never have an end." But trouble lay ahead.

Review and Write

In what ways was the Lewis and Clark Expedition a great adventure for its members?

Across the Continental Divide

Excitement marked the spring and early summer for the Corps of Discovery. A mid-May storm blew one of the pirogues on its side, capsizing much of the party's scientific equipment. Sacajawea, while carrying her baby, rescued much of the supplies and equipment, including some journals. One night, a campfire caught a tree on fire, causing a giant tree limb to crash down on a place where several men had just been sleeping. A few nights later, a buffalo stampeded through camp, just missing the heads of some of the sleeping men.

The men saw no Indians during this part of their journey. But they did see evidence that Indians had once lived in the region, passing abandoned lodges and evidence of a large buffalo hunt. By late May, the expedition passed through a part of the Missouri River where very high cliffs rose along the banks. The soft, sandstone cliffs were strangely shaped, sometimes looking like columns and towers. Come early June, the Missouri became two rivers. Actually, only one of the rivers was the Missouri, but which one? The two leaders decided to each take a group of men and explore the two river choices. On June 13, Captain Lewis heard the sound of the Great Falls of the Missouri River, telling him this was the correct route. He sent word to Clark to join him.

Now the men were forced to haul their equipment and supplies around the 80-foot-high waterfalls. The men built crude carts from cottonwood trees to haul the canoes, but the effort took 24 days to complete. It was backbreaking work, and the men were plagued with prickly pear cactus which grew everywhere and pierced the soles of their moccasins.

Once again, the corps members began seeing signs of their first Indians in some time. Campfires, Indians on horseback off in the distance, Indian dogs—all indicated that Lewis and Clark were going to meet more Native Americans. On July 22, the party reached the Three Forks of the Missouri, where three rivers formed the headwaters of the Missouri River.

Soon, Lewis and Clark encountered the Shoshone Indians, who lived in the Bitterroot Range of the Rockies. In a strange twist of circumstances, one of the first Indians to encounter Lewis was Sacajawea's own brother, Cameahwait! After meeting with the Shoshone, the party received badly needed horses. Cameahwait even presented an old Indian named Toby, a warrior who said he knew the way across the Rockies to the West. It was now August, and the party was in a hurry to reach the Pacific before the onset of winter.

On August 30, the Corps of Discovery set out across the Rockies. This part of the trip was the most difficult journey of all. For nearly two weeks the party faced rock slides, snow falls, dropping temperatures, and food shortages, which led them to eat some of their horses.

But through sheer endurance, the men continued on, crossing the Continental Divide, and reaching western rivers, including the Snake, which flowed into the Columbia, and on to the Pacific Coast. The men spent a miserable winter at the mouth of the Columbia, hoping to see an American ship in the region, but none arrived.

By spring, 1806, Lewis and Clark led their men back to the East, often covering new ground to expand their Indian contacts and their information about the West. Lewis and a party of the men had a violent encounter with a few Blackfoot Indians, which resulted in Lewis killing one of them, the only violent casualty of the entire expedition. The entire party arrived in St. Louis in September, having lost only one man, Sergeant Floyd.

Pike on the Mississippi

The men of the Corps of Discovery covered an extensive expanse of the lands of the Louisiana Purchase. They made contact with over 50 Indian tribes and catalogued nearly 200 species of plants previously unknown to Anglo-Americans in the East. Lewis and Clark added 122 species and subspecies of animals unknown to the scientists of the day.

But it was the land of the Louisiana Purchase which held the most interest for the majority of Americans. And while the men of the Lewis and Clark Expedition were able to map the entire length of the Missouri River and chart the landscape of the northern portion of the territory, they could not cover the land in its entirety. For that reason, others were dispatched into the Louisiana Territory to glean additional information about what exactly the Jefferson administration had purchased from France.

One such additional explorer was an officer named Zebulon Pike. Born in 1779, in New Jersey, Pike had entered military service at age 15 and served under General Anthony Wayne in the Old Northwest. For a time, Pike actually served under the command of his own father, also named Zebulon, who had fought during the American Revolution.

By 1799, young Pike was promoted to lieutenant and was assigned to various western outposts, including Fort Allegheny, Fort Knox, and Kaskaskia. Although Pike's formal education was limited, he was an avid reader who studied military manuals and taught himself mathematics, as well as Spanish and French.

In 1805, while Lewis and Clark were scaling the Rockies with the Corps of Discovery, Pike was ordered to explore an additional portion of the Louisiana Territory. General James Wilkinson ordered Pike to explore the source of the Mississippi River. In August, Pike left St. Louis with 20 soldiers in a 70-foot-long keelboat, bound for the north. Just as Lewis and Clark had been instructed, Pike was to study the possibilities for increased American involvement in the western fur trade, collect minerals and make Indian contacts. In addition, he was to search for possible sites for western forts and invite Indian leaders to visit General Wilkinson in St. Louis.

Pike and his men traveled as far as Little Falls, Minnesota before settling into winter quarters. (Having abandoned the keelboat, Pike's party had continued by sled up the main branch of the Mississippi.) In fact, Pike actually bypassed the true source of the river, Lake Itasca. Pike returned to St. Louis, in April of 1806, having sketched an accurate map of the region. But his mission had limited success. Few chiefs made the pilgrimage to St. Louis and a land agreement he negotiated with the Great Lakes Sioux (Lakota), which included the territory of modern-day St. Paul-Minneapolis, was never ratified by Congress.

But within three months, Pike was sent out again, this time into Louisiana to escort 51 Osage captives back to their homes in western Missouri. General Wilkinson sent about 20 men with Pike, including the general's own son.

Following that mission, he progressed into eastern Nebraska and met with the Pawnees living along the banks of the Republican River. There, Pike was informed that a Spanish army, aware of the American explorer's presence, had been dispatched north from the Spanish Southwest to intercept him.

Already, a Spanish officer, Facundo Melgares had marched 600 Spanish soldiers onto the Great Plains where they had met with the Pawnees, informing them they must remain loyal to Spain. Melgares had handed out Spanish flags to the Pawnees. In time, Pike and the Spanish would cross paths.

Escorted to Santa Fe

Although Pike knew Spanish soldiers were looking for him on the Great Plains, he was not deterred. Just as the Spanish had already done, Pike passed out American flags to the Pawnees, telling them they now lived on American-owned soil. An international incident was brewing on the American western prairies.

Pike continued his journey south, toward Spanish territory. From the Pawnees' encampments, he went into Kansas to the Arkansas River. Although his orders given to him by General Wilkinson had been largely accomplished already, Pike wanted to see more. While on the Arkansas River, he sent some of his troops back to St. Louis, including Wilkinson's son, to report to the general.

Turning to the west, Pike followed the Arkansas in search of its headwaters. On Thanksgiving Day in November of 1806, Pike and his men were in modern-day Colorado, near the site of Colorado Springs. That very day, the men attempted to climb a mountain which would bear their leader's name—Pike's Peak—but failed. The men wore only light cotton clothing, and they were turned back by the cold and snow on the mountain.

Pike pushed his men on, continuing toward Spanish territory. By late December, they were in the vicinity of modern-day Salida, Colorado, and the following month, near the site of Canyon City, still on the banks of the Arkansas River. Pike was in search of the Red River. The Louisiana Purchase described the territory as including the lands drained by the rivers flowing into the Mississippi River. Such rivers as the Missouri, the Platte, the Arkansas, and the Red were included. But south of the Red, it was clearly Spanish territory.

While looking for the Red River (Pike was, in fact, too far west of the actual river's site), the American party crossed the Sangre de Cristo Range of south central Colorado and northern New Mexico, reaching the Rio Grande. Pike, fully aware he was trespassing on Spanish lands, did not turn back. In time, a detachment of 100 Spanish cavalrymen appeared, under the command of Bartolome Fernandez. Pike feigned confusion, explaining he thought he was on the Red River. The Spanish commander ordered Pike to take down the American flag and raise the Spanish emblem over the small stockade which Pike's men had constructed. The American leader was then arrested and taken by Fernandez to the provincial capital at Santa Fe.

Spanish authorities were concerned that Pike was on a spy mission, scouting out Spanish territory for American acquisition. Pike attempted to keep his detailed journal a secret from the Spanish, but it was finally discovered and confiscated. (One hundred years later, the journals of Zebulon Pike were recovered in Mexico City, discovered by a historian doing research in the Mexican archives.)

Despite the tension caused by Pike's presence on Spanish soil, he became friends with the local governor, Joaquin del Rael Alencaster, who provided the American officer with expensive clothing. Pike, however, was ordered to be taken to the Mexican province of Chihuahua, under escort by Fernandez, who had also become friends with Pike. After his arrival in Chihuahua City, Pike was treated with great hospitality by yet another Spanish official, who, in time, released him, allowing him to return to St. Louis in 1807.

Even though Pike's journals had been taken from him, he was able to recount many details from memory. His writings provided new information about yet another portion of the vast lands of the Louisiana Purchase territory. Pike died in 1813, during action in the War of 1812.

Review and Write

1. Why were the Spanish concerned about the presence of Zebulon Pike on their soil?

2. As he explored the interior regions of the American Great Plains, how did Zebulon Pike go beyond the orders he had received from his superior, General Wilkinson?

Test III

Part I.

Matching. *Match the answers shown below with the statements given above. Place the letters of the correct answers in the spaces below.*

1. Fifteenth state admitted to the Union in 1796
2. Original name for Cincinnati, Ohio
3. Name given the violence along the Ohio and Miami Rivers during Cincinnati's early years
4. Trans-Appalachian route financed by U.S. government; a gravel-top road
5. Name for a boat sweep which gave the craft better stability and helped steer downriver
6. Site of the Falls of the Ohio River
7. A large canoe, approximately 50 feet long and eight feet wide; used to carry pioneer family
8. Western keelboat which included a passenger cabin, having same dimensions as standard ark
9. First steamboat used on the Ohio and Mississippi Rivers
10. Canal constructed across New York state between 1817 and 1825
11. Name of Matthias Baldwin's locomotive which reached top speed of 28 miles an hour
12. Name of Robert Fulton's steamboat used on the Hudson River in 1807

A. "the Slaughterhouse"	B. Louisville	C. New Orleans	D. *Old Ironsides*
E. Tennessee	F. gouger	G. Ohio packet boat	H. *Clermont*
I. Losantville	J. National Road	K. pirogue	L. Erie

1. ____ 2. ____ 3. ____ 4. ____ 5. ____ 6. ____ 7. ____ 8. ____ 9. ____ 10. ____ 11. ____ 12. _____

Part II.

Matching. *Match the answers shown below with the statements given above. Place the letters of the correct answers in the spaces below.*

1. American negotiator responsible for the purchase of Louisiana by the United States in 1803
2. President's private secretary who requested command of Corps of Discovery in 1803
3. Site of 1803-04 encampment for the Corps of Discovery before launching up Missouri River
4. Spanish officer who attempted to limit the impact of Zebulon Pike's Great Plains expedition
5. Native American tribe that hosted the Lewis and Clark expedition through winter of 1804-05
6. Native American woman who helped Lewis and Clark expedition through Rockies
7. American officer who gave Zebulon Pike his orders to explore source of Mississippi River
8. Only casualty of the Corps of Discovery; died of appendicitis attack
9. Site of Rocky mountain named for Zebulon Pike
10. Spanish commander who arrested Pike south of Red River; escorted him to Santa Fe
11. Boat commonly used by fur trappers; measured 60 feet by 15 feet with rounded sides
12. New York politician who backed the building of 364-mile-long canal across his state

A. Wood River	B. Sacajawea	C. Colorado Springs	D. DeWitt Clinton
E. Meriwether Lewis	F. Mandans	G. Facundo Melgares	H. mackinaw
I. James Madison	J. Charles Floyd	K. James Wilkinson	L. B. Fernandez

1. ____ 2. ____ 3. ____ 4. ____ 5. ____ 6. ____ 7. ____ 8. ____ 9. ____ 10. ____ 11. ____ 12. _____

48   *The American Frontier*

Tecumseh and the Prophet

While men such as Zebulon Pike and Lewis and Clark helped to spread the news of American dominance over the Louisiana Territory west of the Mississippi during the first decade of the 19th century, some Indians in the Trans-Appalachian East were still resisting the advancement of Anglo-Americans onto their traditional lands.

It was still a time of transition in Indian relations between Eastern tribes and the United States government. President Jefferson was not without sympathy toward the Native Americans. While many Americans saw Indians as just people in the way of American migration and expansion, Jefferson believed in the possibilities of Indian assimilation. Jefferson hoped that Anglo-Americans and Indians could still live side by side; that as the Native American tribes of the East ceded their lands, they would become farmers and take on the culture, work ethic, and social fabric of whites, by living in smaller, tighter farming communities of red-skinned peoples.

To this end, Jefferson supported the abandonment of native cultures in favor of white ways. Although he was not himself a strong advocate for Christianity, he supported missionary efforts to convert the Indians to Christianity. Significant Christian sects dispatched missionaries west to preach the Gospel to the native population. Such Protestant groups as the Baptists, Quakers, Congregationalists, and Presbyterians formed missionary societies in the 1790s, and after 1800, fostering the Christian faith, establishing Indian schools, teaching Native Americans how to read, and encouraging them to abandon their traditional Indian ways. When some Indians converted to Christianity, they caused a split in their tribal structures, bringing about a weakening within their own societies.

Some eastern Native Americans stood in the face of white influences. Some elements among the Shawnee rallied against white influence, led by the warrior Tecumseh and his mystic brother, Tenskwatawa, who was known as "The Prophet."

These tribal leaders saw the future for Native Americans, witnessing Indiana territorial Governor William Henry Harrison sign 15 treaties with various tribes, resulting in their ceding lands to whites, including eastern Michigan, southern Indiana, and nearly all of Illinois between 1801 and 1809.

In 1805, Tenskwatawa began campaigning against cooperation with the white man. He spoke in favor of Indian renewal and spiritual revival. He preached against white influences, including everything from clothing to reliance on manufactured trade goods to the consumption of American alcohol. The Prophet argued for the value of traditional hunting, railed against Indian farming, and told his native audiences they should surrender all privately held property.

As Tenskwatawa gained their emotional support, his brother, Tecumseh, gained their support in forming an Indian resistance movement. Warriors from many different tribes joined with the two Shawnee brothers, helping to create a Northwest Confederation of tribes. Ironically, Tecumseh relied on support from another white power, the British, who, by 1807, were sending food, rifles, and ammunition for the Northwest tribes to use against the encroaching Americans.

When a new American-Indian land agreement, the Treaty of Fort Wayne (1809), resulted in the transfer of 3 million acres of Delaware and Potawatomi land to the territory of Indiana, Tecumseh took his cause to additional tribes, as the lines of conflict became more clearly defined.

Defeat in the Old Southwest

Through his constant message to his fellow Native Americans concerning Indian unity, holding land in common, and resisting further encroachments from whites, Tecumseh was able to gather an extensive following in the Old Northwest Territory. While speaking, the Shawnee leader would hold a tomahawk in his hand and raise it for his audience to see, to make his point concerning Indian cooperation. As he spoke, he would remove his fingers from around the weapon, one by one, until the war axe fell to the ground.

Tecumseh was able to ally tribes from the Southwest to his movement, as well. Among those tribes south of the Ohio River who joined him were various bands of the Choctaws, Chickasaws, Creeks, and Cherokees. But even as Tecumseh was busy gathering more support from such tribes, events turned in his absence. In November, 1811, Governor William Henry Harrison led 1000 soldiers in an attack against the main villages of the Shawnee, including the Indian settlement of Tippecanoe, on the banks of the Wabash River in northern Indiana. Tecumseh's brother, Tenskwatawa rallied 700 Indian warriors into battle against

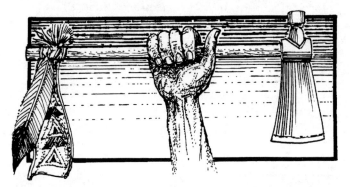

Harrison's forces, and the battle of Tippecanoe resulted in the defeat of the Native Americans, with approximately 150 casualties. Although the battle itself was a Harrison victory, other Indians of the pan-Indian movement later attacked several frontier settlements and killed many whites in Indiana and southern Michigan.

Such events took place on the eve of new conflicts in the Northwest Territory and elsewhere in North America between the United States and Great Britain. In June 1812, President James Madison requested a declaration of war against Britain for its continuous policies of interfering with American shipping on the high seas and their relentless supplying of Northwest tribes against the United States. The war which resulted—called the War of 1812—would involve American and British forces battling against one another on land and at sea. But the violence of the war would also involve several Native American groups, including those supporting Tecumseh. (Since such tribes had already allied themselves with Great Britain, it was difficult for Indians not to become part of the war in some way or another.)

In the early days of the conflict, the British and their Indian allies, including Tecumseh, did well against the Americans on several different battle fronts. When Americans marched against Canada, the British-Indian alliance defeated them repeatedly. In July 1812, an American army led by General William Hull of Michigan was badly beaten, and 2000 of Hull's men were captured. The British followed up their victory by capturing Fort Dearborn (now Chicago) and Detroit.

One of the few bright spots for the Americans during the first year of the war was the recapture of Fort Detroit by an American force led by William Henry Harrison. Harrison later defeated a combined force of British and Indians in the battle of the Thames, on October 5, 1813. During that battle, Tecumseh, fighting alongside the British, was killed, ending much of the core of the pan-Indian movement in the Northwest and Southwest. His death effectively destroyed the alliance of tribes united against the Americans in the Northwest Territory.

In addition, when General Andrew Jackson campaigned against the Creeks in the Southwest, defeating them in the March 1814 battle of Horseshoe Bend, killing 800 Indians, the days of Indian resistance to white movement east of the Mississippi River came to an effective end.

A West in Transition

By defeating the Creeks in the Southwest, General Andrew Jackson was able to extract a new series of land cessions by Native Americans to the American government. Under the Treaty of Fort Jackson (1814), the Creeks surrendered 23 million acres of traditional lands, half of those claimed by the tribe's leaders. When Jackson forced such significant concessions from the Creeks, they gave the Tennessee Indian fighter a new name— Sharp Knife.

By 1815, the War of 1812 was over, the British had been stalemated into a treaty, and the Americans felt they had vindicated themselves against challenges issuing from Great Britain before the war. The various Indian coalition groups, including the one led by Tecumseh before the war, came crashing down like a house of cards. With any serious Indian challenge eliminated after the War of 1812, the way West was once again open for thousands of Americans.

With Kentucky and Tennessee already largely settled, this new wave of American migrants focused their sights on the Old Northwest and the Old Southwest. The transition of Americans into the West is revealed by the numbers. According to the 1790 national census, 95 percent of America's population lived in the Atlantic seaboard states. But by 1820, one out of every four Americans lived west of the Appalachians.

As with other massive migrations to the West, this one can be explained, as well. Population pressures in the East caused many to move into the interior. The American population nearly doubled in twenty years, between 1800 and 1820 (from 5.3 to 9.6 million). The lack of available farm land caused many to move West where land was available and cheap. This meant that 2.5 million Americans were calling the West home by 1820.

The role played by this factor of inexpensive land was a significant one. Under the Land Ordinance of 1785, the government had made lands available for purchase at the rate of a dollar an acre. Since the ordinance required settlers to purchase no less than 640 acres, or one square mile of territory, the price was prohibitive, since many would-be farmers did not have enough money. Typically, such lands were purchased by land speculators intent on reselling the land at a profit, and dividing it into smaller parcels.

In time, the government caught on to the problem it had created for frontiersmen seeking to purchase western land. Under the Land Act of 1820, the government agreed to sell western lands at a price of $1.25 an acre but in plots as small as 80 acres (rather than the 640-acre minimum). This was a workable system, only requiring a cash outlay of $100 for the land-hungry pioneer farmer.

As Americans moved into the far western reaches of the Trans-Appalachian region, they typically followed one of five popular routes west. Former New Englanders used the Mohawk and Genesee Turnpike, extending across New York to Lake Erie. Lake travel delivered them into Ohio. Those travelling from Pennsylvania or the Middle States used the Lancaster Turnpike from Philadelphia to Pittsburgh, then floated down the Ohio River. Others bound west from Virginia or Maryland might follow the National Road that began in Baltimore. Finally, Southerners still used the Wilderness Road and the Saluda-Cumberland Gap, just as Daniel Boone had decades earlier. Those from South Carolina or Georgia utilized the Federal Road which ran south, scooting around the southern end of the Appalachians into the western lands of modern-day Alabama and Mississippi

Review and Write

1. What important result was gained by the defeat of the Creeks in the Southwest by General Andrew Jackson? Who gained from the result and who lost?

2. What were the five basic land routes used as Americans moved into the Trans-Appalachian west? Where were the routes located?

Upheaval in the Gulf Plains

One of the later phases of the Trans-Appalachian movement was the migration of Americans into the Old Southwest, the lands compromising the modern-day states of Mississippi and Alabama.

The region, known as the Gulf Plains province was dramatically different from the lands comprising the Old Northwest. Generally it included territory extending along the Gulf of Mexico from Florida to the lower banks of the Rio Grande, taking the shape of a triangle or pyramid, its apex centered in the vicinity of the juncture of the Ohio and Mississippi Rivers.

The land features prairies with rich soils, where timber was still available in abundance, but supporting different trees than those found in the Old Northwest or even east of the Appalachians. The Gulf Plains forests were thick with hardwood in the north, pine trees in its center, and cypress and pine in the tidal lands of the Gulf Coast.

The climate of the Gulf Plains held the key to its future as an agricultural region. This relatively mild environment was highly suitable to the cultivation of cotton, which requires a growing season of about 200 days, with little threat of frost on either end of the season. Cotton cultivation in the spring requires moist, warm weather, while the summer temperatures need to be hot and dry, as the cotton bolls ripen. The Gulf Plains feature just this combination of weather pattern.

The Gulf Plains were late in development given the endurance of the Native Americans of the region. Four tribes dominated the plains country: the Creeks, Chickasaw, Choctaw, and Cherokee. As late as 1830, the tribes still boasted 60,000 people east of the Mississippi River.

The Creeks and Cherokee lived in Georgia and Alabama territory. They held massive acreage of traditional lands, including 10 million acres in Georgia and six million in Alabama. The Chickasaw and Choctaw claimed over 1 million acres in Alabama and 16 million in Mississippi.

With a continuing contact and influence exerted by Anglo-Americans, these Native Americans had developed into viable farmers, taking on many aspects of white culture and practice. Indian villages might be similar to white towns and settlements, complete with houses, farms, orchards, blacksmith shops, and other indicators of Indian assimilation. These tribes raised large acreage of corn, kept herds of cattle and hogs, and grew cotton with black slaves providing the work force. They used modern tools, rifles, spinning wheels, and looms—even built gristmills for grinding their grain into flour.

Perhaps no tribe of the region had become as assimilated as had the Cherokee. Their adaptations of white culture and influence ran through every level of Cherokee civilization. According to the 1824 national census, the Cherokee operated 18 schools, owned 36 gristmills, 13 sawmills, 762 looms, over 2,400 spinning wheels, 172 wagons, nearly 3,000 plows, 7,600 horses, 22,000 head of cattle, 46,000 hogs, 62 blacksmith shops, nine stores, two tanning facilities producing leather, and a mill to produce gunpowder.

The Cherokee dressed in white men's clothing, developed a written language, printed their own newspaper, and even wrote their own constitution. Many of them had converted to Christianity through the efforts of missionaries. They built roads, turnpikes, and ferries to service people across bridgeless rivers. The Choctaw and Chickasaw had made similar strides prior to 1830, as well, in becoming similar to Anglo-American culture in every way possible. But such changes would not protect these tribes from white intrusion and destruction.

Review and Write

1. How were the Cherokee different from their Native American neighbors?

2. Describe the region of the Gulf Plains. Where is it located? What are some of the notable features of the region?

The Cherokee Fight for Survival

Men such as Thomas Jefferson, a retired public figure in the 1820s, praised the Indian assimilation that was accomplished by the Cherokee, Chickasaw and Choctaw. He had always hoped the answer to the nation's Indian problems would be found in the assimilation of the Native Americans.

Ironically, as these Southeastern tribes became more and more similar to Anglo-Americans, it caused alarm among various state governments and their white citizens. It was the goal of the leaders of such states, and of the federal government, as well, to remove Indian land claims in the Southeast, despite the number of ways the Native Americans of the region had adapted to and adopted white ways and values. The reality was this—no matter how such tribes as the Cherokee might make themselves similar to whites, they remained Native Americans. The common prejudices of the day would not allow these Indians equal legal status with whites.

By the 1820s, the government began to systematically destroy Indian land claims. In 1825, President James Monroe ordered American agents to obtain a land cession from a portion of the Creek bands. This was accomplished by out-and-out bribery. A faction of the Creeks agreed to cede the territory in question, but not the majority of the Creeks themselves. Nevertheless, the treaty was approved by the U.S. Senate and the federal government ceded the former Creek lands to the state of Georgia.

During these same years, the Cherokee of Georgia were being pressured to surrender their traditional lands in Georgia, which they were unwilling to do. When the state of Georgia pushed its claims against the Cherokee, these civilized Native Americans did not turn to armed conflict; instead, they took the state of Georgia to court.

Cherokee leaders appealed to the United States Supreme Court for an injunction to stop Georgian confiscation of Indian lands under state law. The Supreme Court agreed in favor of the Cherokee. Lawyers for the Cherokee claimed they were a sovereign nation located within the United States, and, thus, not subject to state law or authority.

In the Supreme Court decision, *Cherokee Nation v. Georgia*, the Court, led by Chief Justice John Marshall, determined that the Cherokee did not have jurisdiction in the case. The Cherokee were defined neither as a foreign nor a domestic state, but as a "domestic dependent nation," which did not give them power to bring suits into a federal court against the United States.

In another landmark case challenging the Georgia laws which limited Cherokee land ownership, titled *Worcester v. Georgia*, the Court decided that the laws of Georgia had no binding on the Cherokee residents living in parts of that southern state. This decision infuriated the governor of Georgia. Also, the president of the United States, Andrew Jackson, refused to abide by the Supreme Court decision.

Even with such supportive Supreme Court decisions, however, the tribes of the Southeast were unable to retain their traditional lands. Instead, the states passed additional laws, confiscating Indian lands, and imposing penalties against any and all who might publicly oppose tribal land grabs by these same state governments.

The days of the tribes in the Southeast appeared near an end. In fact, President Andrew Jackson, elected in 1828, had campaigned on the removal of the Indian presence from the territory east of the Mississippi. Expulsion was to become the key to the government's new Indian policy on the frontier.

The Indian Removal

The policy of Indian removal was not new with the rise of Andrew Jackson as president. Even President Jefferson, who had been a strong advocate of assimilation of Native Americans, centered in their adoption of white ways including a reliance on farming, had promoted Indian removal as an alternative for any tribe that did not want to adopt a "non-Indian" lifestyle. His plan called for those Indians who chose, to be relocated west of the Mississippi River in the government's Indian Territory, located within the modern-day states of Oklahoma, Kansas, and Nebraska.

Those national leaders who followed Jefferson as president also tended to follow his dualistic plan—either assimilation or removal. The Northwest Territory was emptied of most of its native population following the War of 1812. Jackson, during the 1830s, worked to relocate Southeastern tribes such as the Cherokee, Chickasaw, Choctaw, and Creek into the same open region, away from Anglo-American migration and settlement.

In 1830, Congress passed Jackson's proposed Indian Removal Act, whose purpose was to provide funding for delivering Indians from their traditional homes to reserve lands in the West. With the defeat of the Cherokees in court, there was little the Southeastern tribes could do but agree to move to their new homes.

Some tribes fought back, however. The Seminoles of Florida, with help from runaway black slaves, hid in the Florida Everglades, fighting a guerrilla war against the U.S. Army. The Seminole leader behind this resistance was Chief Osceola. For seven years, Osceola led his people, hiding women and children and encouraging his fighters to hit and run against a stronger enemy. After a government expenditure of $40 million and the lives of 1500 federal troops, the government gave up. In the end, the Seminole resistance was a success. However, some did relocate.

Throughout the 1830s, Southeastern tribes packed up their belongings and moved into the Indian Reserve. The Choctaws surrendered their lands in 1830, under the Treaty of Dancing Rabbit Creek and agreed to move to a reserve west of the Arkansas Territory. The Creeks ceded their lands from 1832 through 1834, and completed their move West by 1836.

One of the last to move were the Cherokees. By 1835, they had signed a treaty which surrendered nearly all of their lands. But the treaty was made between the U.S. government and a minority faction of the tribe's leaders. Nevertheless, the Cherokee would be forced to move, even though the majority of its leaders had not signed the removal treaty.

During the winter of 1838–39, U.S. Army troops rounded up the Cherokee, approximately 13,000 to 17,000 of them, and ordered them to make a forced march through winter snows to the Indian Territory of Oklahoma. A miserable move, often referred to now as the "Trail of Tears," thousands of Cherokees died en route. When the Cherokee arrived in Oklahoma, the majority leaders of the tribe tracked down the minority tribal representatives who had agreed with American authorities about the removal and ordered their executions.

While nearly all of the tribe was removed to the West, about 1000 Cherokees managed to elude U.S. authorities and escaped into the Great Smoky Mountains of western North Carolina where they became known as the "Eastern Band of Cherokee." In time—once American authorities decided to let them remain—they purchased land from the government. With the policy of Indian removal, the frontier was open to Anglo-American movement clear to the Mississippi River.

Review and Write

How was Chief Osceola able to fight an effective campaign of resistance against the U.S. Army for so long? What was the outcome of his resistance?

Moving Across the South

Even before the Indian Removal Act of 1830 brought about the reluctant, even forced, migration of Southeastern Native American tribes into the West, the lands of the Old Southwest were filling up with pioneering migrants and southern farmers expanding the cultivation of short-staple cotton.

The rise in short-staple cotton growing in the south had taken off following the invention of a device built by a northerner named Eli Whitney in 1793. Whitney was working as a tutor for a southern plantation mistress named Catherine Greene whose former husband, Nathaniel Greene, was a hero of the American Revolution.

One of America's most innovative inventors and tinkerers, Whitney had built a hand-cranked device with rows of metal "teeth" that separated the green, sticky seeds (the short-staples) from the white, cotton lint. This simple device eliminated the bottleneck of cotton production, namely, how to clean the cotton quickly and efficiently. Whitney's Cotton Gin (short for engine) could clean 50 pounds of cotton in one day. By hand, cleaning one pound of cotton had required a full day's labor.

With his innovative device, Whitney demonstrated that growing short-staple cotton could be profitable. In less than a generation, slaveholders in Georgia and South Carolina alone were producing 60 million pounds of cotton a year. But cotton was a crop that quickly wore out the soil. Without adding fertilizers, cotton sapped the minerals from the soil in a cycle of about five to eight years. Thus, in the early decades of the 19th century, southern cotton producers were in search of new land for cotton cultivation.

This mass migration west across the Gulf Plains was concentrated in the "black belt," the name given the fertile regions of Georgia, Alabama, and Mississippi. After the War of 1812, with the subjugation of various Indian tribes, people flocked into Alabama by the thousands. Many brought along their slaves who cleared new land for cotton and corn fields, drained swamps, cut the piney woods, and sowed fields for the first crops.

The numbers tell the migration story. In just ten years (1810-20), Mississippi grew in non-Indian population from 31,000 to nearly 75,000. In Alabama, the boom was even greater, causing growth from approximately 9000 to a staggering 144,000 during the same ten-year period. Many of these southern migrants came from South Carolina. In fact, by 1850, about 125,000 South Carolinians had moved out of their home state into Georgia, Alabama, or Mississippi.

Following the initial stage of movement into Alabama and Mississippi, additional mass migrations occurred in later decades. With the removal of Southeastern tribes during the 1830s, the region was once again open to further Anglo-American movement. Between 1832 and 1838, a surge of southern movement took place and another burst occurred again in the mid-1850s.

Cotton cultivation remained the economic backbone of much of the western movement across the frontier regions of the Gulf Plains. Cotton planting even expanded across the Mississippi into the western territories of Louisiana and Texas.

Such massive movement allowed for a quick transition of southern territories into states. By 1821, Alabama, Mississippi, Louisiana, as well as Missouri, had completed the process of becoming states. A generation later, additional states were formed out of Texas and Florida.

New Agriculture on the Frontier

With the development of steamboats, extensive canal systems, and the coming of the railroads, Americans everywhere began experiencing a transportation boom. The impact of the Industrial Revolution was having a distinct effect on the daily lives of everyone, from factory worker to urban dweller to farm worker. In fact, since most Americans were involved directly in agriculture in the first half of the 19th century, it was this socio-economic group that was most significantly affected by industrialization.

Such changes trickled to the farming level in sometimes extremely simple, yet straightforward ways. The developments in transportation, for example, brought the farmers better roads and new means of shipping their produce and livestock to market—whether on a canal boat, train car, or a steam packet on the Mississippi River. Such transportation also sped up the process of transforming the frontier into a series of civilized settlements on the American landscape. By the 1830s, following the opening of the Erie Canal, pioneers flooded into the Old Northwest (Ohio, Indiana, Illinois, Michigan, and Wisconsin), and even found their way further west to Iowa.

This great movement and occupation of the Old Northwest helped to further develop the economic centers of Trans-Appalachian regions, turning frontier towns into cities. In return, those cities developed into economic outposts noted for a specialization in their local production and agriculture. Farmers in Ohio became noted for their crops of corn and their corn-fed hogs. By 1840, Ohio had also become the center of America's wheat production. Again, the Erie Canal played a role, as Midwestern-produced wheat was shipped across central New York to eastern urban centers, especially New York City, to feed the ever-increasing numbers of European immigrants arriving by the thousands throughout much of the decade to follow.

In addition, significant changes in the mechanization of farming altered the work of farmers. New tools and equipment turned western farmers into extremely productive workers. An inventor named John Deere developed a cold steel plow in 1837, whose blade could cut through the thickest root system without allowing the stickiest soil to adhere to it. Other machines, such as seed drillers, had an impact on agriculture, as well.

Perhaps the most significant mechanics applied to farming were embodied in a threshing machine invented by Cyrus McCormick. Patented in 1834, McCormick's mechanical reaping device cut the time required to bring in a fall harvest of grain. Earlier, when the work was done by hand, it would

require an entire day for one man, armed with a cradle scythe, to cut two, maybe three acres of wheat. But with the reaper, drawn by horse power, the same farmer could cut up to twelve acres from sun to sun.

With the development, then, of a more industrialized system, the frontier of the Trans-Appalachian region began to disappear, just as it had three or four generations earlier in most of the original thirteen colonies along the Atlantic Coast. However, the frontier era was not coming to an end. While such regions as the Old Northwest and the Old Southwest had been primitive, underpopulated, untapped, and remote in early decades, by 1840, those lands were organized, established, well-populated, mechanized, and charted.

And with the movement of more and more Americans west of the Mississippi, new frontiers lay ahead.

Trade Along the Santa Fe Trail

During the decades between 1820 and 1860, as Americans east of the Mississippi River busied themselves filling in the landscape, they built new routes across the interior, such as the National Road, which eventually extended to St. Louis, Missouri, west of the Mississippi. But at the same time the frontier was pushing closer and closer to the Mississippi, some Americans were already west of the great river, establishing trade in the Trans-Mississippi West. Early routes across the Great Plains of this new West included the Santa Fe Trail.

The Santa Fe Trail connected Missouri settlers, traders, and businessmen with their Mexican counterparts in the bustling frontier town of Santa Fe, located in the northern portion of modern-day New Mexico. Beginning in 1821, Americans regularly used the trail. Prior to that year, most Anglo-Americans were not well received in Santa Fe. The colonial Spanish government in the northern provinces feared the arrival of Americans and looked at each arrival with suspicion. The American explorer, Zebulon Pike, had run into trouble with Spanish authorities in New Mexico when he wandered into Spanish territory during an expedition in 1807.

But in 1821, the Mexican people successfully carried out a revolution against the Spanish. Once Mexico was firmly in Mexican hands, the trading town of Santa Fe was opened to American traders. One of the first on the scene, ready to make the most of the opportunity, was a Missouri resident named William Becknell. He arrived in Santa Fe on November 16, 1821, with wagonloads of trade goods which the Mexicans eagerly bought, providing Becknell with a handsome profit.

Even with the opening of trade with Americans, the Santa Fe Trail itself was not well defined in 1821, due to infrequent use. Becknell had started out in Franklin, Missouri, and crossed the treeless plains between the Kansas and Arkansas Rivers. Once he reached the foothills of the southern Rocky Mountains, he made a turn to the southwest, cutting across the southern corner of modern-day Colorado. Later, a post was erected at that juncture, called Bent's Fort. This station provided travelers a welcome stopping place until it burned in 1849.

From there, Becknell continued on until he reached the outpost settlement of Santa Fe. Most traders who followed after Becknell used this same general route, which became well-worn with time. Later traders, intent on shortening time on the trail, developed shortcuts, such as the Cimarron Cutoff from Fort Dodge, Kansas, to the Mora River in New Mexico.

Traders on the Santa Fe Trail used Conestoga wagons to carry their trade goods. They needed large wagons capable of hauling heavy freight. Typically, such traders moved in wagon trains, circling the wagons at night to provide shelter and security from Indians, some of whom resented the movement of American wagons across their traditional lands.

Among the trade goods delivered to Santa Fe were cotton goods, woolens, hardware, and china. In exchange, the Missouri traders often returned with horses, mules, beaver skins, buffalo robes, and silver, which was in great demand in the United States. Trade on the trail peaked in 1843, when 3,000 American wagons carried $500,000 worth of trade goods to Santa Fe.

For a solid generation, the Santa Fe Trail provided a viable trade connection between Americans and Mexicans. But when the Mexican War erupted in the 1840s, this form of international trade was halted.

Review and Write

1. What circumstances allowed the development of trade along the Santa Fe Trail?

2. How did the Santa Fe Trail connect the markets of the Missouri economy and the former Spanish settlement of Santa Fe? Why did trade remain limited as long as the Spanish were in power?

Western Fur Trade

Within 50 years of the election of George Washington as the first Chief Executive of the United States, the land east of the Mississippi was not only occupied, but organized, as well. By 1840, the entire region from the Atlantic to the Mississippi River had been carved into states, except for Florida and Wisconsin.

Just as Americans had moved west in great numbers between 1790 and 1840, so they continued to move beyond the Mississippi River, out onto the Great Plains country. As settlers and adventurers eyed the vast, open expanses at the heart of the North American continent, they searched for opportunities to establish themselves in this new world. One such opportunity lay in the western development of the fur trade.

Just as fur had proven a viable resource in other sections of North America during other eras, so fur—primarily beaver—was again to become the dominant attraction, luring trappers, traders, businessmen, and the legendary mountain men into the region's remotest corners. Portions of the Trans-Mississippi West were claimed by the British, the Spanish, the Russians and now the Americans. Each based a part of its presence in the western wilderness on the fur industry.

Three important fur "capitals" developed in the West in the early 1800s. The British base was Fort Vancouver, located on the lower Columbia River, opposite the mouth of the Willamette River. The post was built by the Hudson's Bay Company in 1824. From this location, the British could control the trade of the entire Columbia valley, including the Snake River and the Willamette Valley.

The Spanish centered their fur trade in the small settlement of Taos, just 100 miles north of Santa Fe, while the American fur center was St. Louis. This community lay at the mouth of the Missouri River. From here, and from the Spanish base at Taos, American fur trappers and mountain men set out for the mountainous country of the Rockies. By the early 1820s, American trappers used the rendezvous system developed by Americans in St. Louis and by the British at Fort Vancouver. Using this new method, the old system of trading posts near Indian populations was abandoned. In its place, non-Indian trappers did their own trapping, rather than trade with the Indians, who had historically been responsible for bringing in furs.

The pattern established by the mid-1820s became the norm. A party of perhaps 100 trappers was dispatched into the West by a fur company. Once they arrived in the region of the Rockies, the men split off in brigades, each going its own way in search of beaver. The trapping season stretched between autumn until the next June or July. This was the time of year when the animals' furs were the thickest.

The mountain men were a tough breed, living entirely on a daily diet of five to eight pounds of, often, raw meat. They took on an Indian appearance and risked death almost every day. By July or August, a "rendezvous" of the various brigades was held at a predetermined place. The annual rendezvous was a raucous event, complete with wild drinking, frolicking, and repeated fights. Indians were often present, as well.

Here the mountain men brought in their furs, selling them to their company's representatives. In exchange, the mountain man would buy his supplies for the next season, including gunpowder, lead, traps, salt, trade items, and whiskey. Often, after purchasing his needs for the next trapping season, the mountain man might have nothing left to show for his year's efforts. A significant contribution made by mountain men was a greater knowledge of the geography of the West.

Review and Write

During the first 50 years of American expansion into the West, the years between 1790 and 1840, the reach of the United States had extended to what western lands?

Americans and Manifest Destiny

When Europeans arrived in North America, they established settlements along the Atlantic Coast, rarely moving further than 50 miles inland. This remained the case for most of a century and a half. But once Americans moved west of the Appalachian Mountains, they never stopped until they eventually reached the Pacific Coast. What drove pioneers, frontiersmen, farmers, and others to claim the entire distance between these two great oceans for themselves? How did the lands that today comprise the United States come to be dominated by Americans, instead of the British, French, Spanish, Russians, or even the Native Americans who had arrived thousands of years earlier?

One factor which determined that the Trans-Mississippi West would be part of an "American West" was in the rapid movement of migration throughout the latter decades of the 18th century and most of the 19th century. When President Jefferson facilitated the purchase of the Louisiana Territory from the French in 1803, he estimated that it would require one hundred generations of Americans to claim and settle the entire region. In reality, it took only four. For all the decades the English colonists were content to remain settled along the Atlantic seaboard, 19th-century Americans were restless, constantly in motion and greedy for land.

While the Louisiana Purchase did bring a vast territory of over 800,000 square miles under the jurisdiction of the U.S. government, it was a risk to move further west to places such as Texas, Arizona, California, or Utah—places claimed and occupied by European powers, such as Great Britain and Spain. Yet Americans seemed prepared to risk war and death to make the North American continent truly American.

To justify the occupation of lands which were claimed by others, Americans developed a philosophy which sometimes bordered on a religion, a concept known as "manifest destiny."

The term was coined in 1845 by then newspaperman John O'Sullivan who wrote: "Our manifest destiny [is] to overspread and possess the whole of the continent which Providence [God] has given us for the free development of the great experiment of liberty and . . . self-government." To O'Sullivan, it was the destiny, determined by God, for Americans to spread themselves and their democratic tendencies throughout the West, regardless of thousands of Mexicans and Indians living there.

Armed with the fervor of manifest destiny, Americans made their way west. Texas became a state in the Union in 1845, despite the wishes of the Mexican government, which had owned Texas. Before the end of the 1840s, the United States would fight and win a war against Mexico and lay claim to the Southwest from Colorado to California. Great Britain would surrender its claim to the Oregon Country, promoting Americans to stream into the fertile region by the wagonload. And when gold was discovered in the tailrace of a saw mill in California on a Swiss immigrant's ranch, nothing about the West would ever be the same again.

Review and Write

Why did the Trans-Mississippi migration pose a risk for Americans during its earlier years?

The Opening of Texas

The year 1821 was a watershed date in the history of the American Southwest. During that fateful year, dissatisfied and oppressed Mexicans rose up and overthrew their longtime masters, the Spanish. With the northern provinces dramatically underpopulated, the new Mexican government was intent on settling these vast regions by any means possible. They opened up territories such as Tejas (pronounced tay-HAAS, the Spanish spelling of Texas) to immigration by non-Mexicans. The region was home to not more then three or four thousand residents, centered in three concentrated communities. Nearly all those who responded to the opportunity for free Mexican land were the Americans living on the frontier.

One of the first Americans to receive a significant land grant of 18,000 acres in Tejas was a Missourian named Moses Austin. When Austin died suddenly, the grant was transferred to his son, Stephen F. Austin. He became the first American land agent, called an empresario, in Mexican-controlled Tejas. Thousands followed him into this land of opportunity. One incentive to move to the West was an economic depression in the United States, called the Panic of 1819, which dispossessed some Americans and caused severe economic problems for most.

Unlike the typical American frontier experience, which often included the occupation of land to which pioneers and immigrants did not have legal title, the American movement into Tejas was almost entirely legal. Austin and other later empresarios distributed their property to eager American residents, people intent on making a new life in the Trans-Mississippi West.

The land grants doled out by Mexican authorities were generous, indeed. Under an 1823 law, empresarios were given a grant if they agreed to help 200 families immigrate to Tejas and occupy land. The empresario distributed land according to its intended use. If the new arrival was to farm it, he would receive 177 acres, called a labor. If he intended to raise cattle, he was granted 4,428

acres, known as a sitio. Since there was little difference between the types of land granted in either case other than the number of acres, most American immigrants stated they intended to raise cattle.

However, there were some strings attached to claiming land in Tejas. The Mexican government required all immigrants to become citizens of Mexico and to convert to Catholicism. Typically, American colonists agreed to these requirements in name only.

Originally, the Mexican government expected its offer of free land in Tejas would attract people from around the world, including Mexicans, Europeans, and Americans. But few others, except for Americans, answered the call. While no reliable numbers exist, it is estimated that by 1830, about 30,000 people were living in Tejas, and all were Americans, except for about 4,000 native Mexicans. As the American population in Tejas swelled, Mexican authorities began to panic. Then, an American empresario, Hayden Edwards, following a dispute with local Mexican officials, attempted a revolution establishing the Republic of Fredonia. Although the attempted revolt was defeated quickly by Mexican troops, along with support from Stephen Austin, the Mexicans were certain they would have to take drastic steps in the future to keep Tejas from coming under complete American control. The heavy-handed changes taking place in Tejas would, ironically, cause another revolution, and this one would succeed.

Review and Write

1. What incentives might have attracted Americans to Tejas?

2. Why was the year 1821 such a significant year in the history of the American Southwest? What events helped set the stage for the direction of the region in years to follow?

Revolution Comes to Texas

Following the Hayden Edwards revolution, the Mexican government began searching for a way to limit American power in Tejas. Although Edwards did not have popular support from American landholders, and was himself expelled from Tejas, the Mexicans remained unsure of what course to follow.

It did not help calm the Mexican mindset concerning a growing distrust of the Americans living in Tejas when the United States government made repeated overtures to purchase Tejas from Mexico. In 1825, 1827, and 1829, both formal and informal proposals for an American acquisition were floated, and all were summarily turned down by the Mexican government.

By 1830, a desperate Mexico had a plan. On April 6, the Mexican Congress adopted a law which closed the Tejas frontier to further American immigration and colonization. It also banned the importation of additional black slaves into the province. But with the Mexican capital more than 1000 miles away, there was no way such a law could be enforced. The Tejas frontier was so extensive, new arrivals could not possibly be monitored.

Tension and antagonism continued to rise between the Americans and the Mexicans. Under the 1824 Mexican Constitution, the buying and selling of slaves was banned. In addition, all marriages were to be performed by a Catholic priest. Since nearly all the Americans living in Tejas were Protestants (despite their "conversions" to the Catholic faith), such a stipulation was not popular. Further, the Mexican government declared that all children born in non-Catholic families would be denied the rights of inheritance. Such steps widened the differences between the Americans and their Mexican leaders.

By 1833, a new president of Mexico came to power by military force—Antonio Lopez de Santa Anna, a general in the Mexican army. Santa Anna made few concessions to the Americans and was unpopular as a leader. When Stephen Austin made a trip to Mexico City to speak on behalf of American concerns, he received little from an entrenched

Mexican government. When he attempted to return to Texas, he was arrested by Mexican police on charges that he had penned a letter saying that if Tejas did not receive independence from Mexico, the province would rise up and separate on its own. He remained in a Mexican jail until 1835.

In the meantime, Mexican officials in Tejas were clamping down on the non-payment of import duties by Americans. Santa Anna, in fact, dispatched a Mexican army to Tejas to enforce the collection of customs duties. American smuggling was rampant at the time, amounting to over 200,000 pesos annually. Antagonism developed and open defiance of Mexican authorities in Tejas became commonplace.

By 1835, Tejas was seething with rebellion. Other Mexican provinces, a half dozen altogether, were also chaffing under Santa Anna's rule, ready for revolution. In Tejas, violence first erupted due to a practical joke. Under Mexican law, all exports were to be inspected by Mexican agents. An American, Andrew Briscoe, filled a box with sawdust and marked it for export. He gathered a crowd of associates to watch while an official opened the box, finding it filled with the useless material. When the bystanders mocked the Mexican agent, he attempted to arrest Briscoe. A fight broke out, Mexican soldiers were summoned, and tensions mounted. With an army on its way, Tejanos began rallying, including Stephen Austin. By the fall of 1835, the Texas Revolution was underway.

The Texans Defend Themselves

When the Texas Revolution began, it was not due to cruelty or absolute tyranny on the part of the Mexican dictator, General Santa Anna. That view soon became part of the folklore attached to the Texas effort. Without question, the Mexican administration of Texas had been weak, limited, and the central government of Mexico had ruled in chaotic fashion.

But the Texas revolt was caused largely by the earlier Mexican mistake of admitting Americans, who, through earlier frontier experiences, were unruly and aggressive men. Such men never accepted the authority of the Mexican government over them. As long as the Mexicans exerted limited control and otherwise looked the other way when American immigrants ignored Mexican law, the relationship between host and guest remained non-confrontational. When authorities attempted to reestablish their authority in Texas, by sending tax agents, customs collectors, and soldiers, the Texans interpreted such steps as a challenge, leading them to take up arms against Mexico.

The Texas Revolution received immediate support from the people of the United States. Nearly every American hoped their fellow Americans in Texas would be successful in their efforts. The United States government, however, maintained a low profile of support.

With a Mexican army headed for Texas in the fall of 1835, Texans gathered at a convention on October 15, at a site called Washington-on-the-Brazos (River). Stephen Austin was already campaigning for moderation, but it was becoming clear to him that the possibilities for reconciliation with Mexico were slipping away. He wrote a letter which circulated through the American settlements: "War is our only recourse. We must defend our rights, ourselves, and our country, by force of arms." But Austin's letter did not mention independence for Texas, and most of the delegates at the convention sided with Austin, who retained hope that the antagonisms between Mexico and Texas might be worked out. The members of the convention left open the possibilities of remaining a part of Mexico.

But a Mexican army continued to march on Texas. Some Texans were led by James Bowie. Born in Tennessee, Bowie was a colonel in the Texas Rangers and was known for his heavy drinking. (While his name is linked historically to the "Bowie Knife" he was probably not its inventor.) As a Mexican army approached the community of San Antonio de Bexar, Bowie led 100 men out to meet them and captured a Mexican pack train outside the town.

When the Mexican army arrived, under the command of General Martin Perfecto de Cos, in December 1835, Bowie and his men captured them during the siege of San Antonio. Bowie agreed to allow Cos and his men to return to Mexico on the condition they not take up arms against the Texans again. Cos promised, but, after his release, he later returned as a column commander under General Santa Anna.

Throughout 1835, while the Texans had debated their future and their immediate goals—whether to reconcile with Mexico or fight for independence—President-General Santa Anna had taken advantage of his opportunity to settle revolutions in other Mexican provinces. Typically, he established a local strong man as the governor, ending local rebellion, such as in California. Elsewhere, he used military force. By early 1836, General Santa Anna was able to focus on entirely on Texas. He led an army of 5000, arriving at San Antonio on February 23, 1836, where a small group of Texans had barricaded themselves inside a local mission called the Alamo.

Review and Write

1. How did Stephen Austin change his position concerning the growing Texas Revolution?

2. Why was it a mistake for the Mexican government to allow Americans to move into Mexican-held Texas? When the Mexicans tried to reestablish authority in Texas, how did the Texans react?

The Siege at the Alamo

The Alamo was a Spanish mission built in 1718. It was originally called San Antonio de Valero, but came to be known as the "Alamo," the Spanish word for cottonwood trees which originally clustered around the mission grounds.

With the approach of General Santa Anna's army, a handful of Texans prepared to meet the enemy by taking refuge in the old mission. The town had about 150 Texans, under the command of Lieutenant Colonel William Barret Travis. He and his men had occupied the Alamo when the revolution had broken out against Mexican authorities. (Mexican army personnel had used the Alamo as their military headquarters in San Antonio de Bexar prior to the revolution.)

During the final days of January 1836, Travis and his men became aware of the approach of Santa Anna's army toward San Antonio. Texas General Sam Houston, a former Tennessee governor and friend of President Andrew Jackson, ordered Travis to abandon the Alamo and blow it up before the Mexicans arrived. But after Colonel James Bowie delivered the message, the decision was made to defend the site instead. It was to be a fatal mistake for the Texans.

Before Santa Anna arrived, a group of Kentuckians, led by legendary frontiersman, Colonel David Crockett reached the Alamo on February 8. As the men prepared for the inevitable attack, antagonism broke out between the leaders in the Alamo. When a ranking colonel named Neill left his men, putting himself on a "twenty days' leave," quarrels erupted between Travis and Jim Bowie. Bowie resented Travis, who considered the hot-headed Bowie to be nothing more than a drunk. In time, the two men agreed to share command of the garrison. However, Bowie became ill, leaving Travis in complete command.

By late February, General Santa Anna arrived with approximately 6,000 men. He immediately ordered the men inside the Alamo to surrender, but Travis refused, answering the Mexican order by firing a cannon. The 187 men barricaded inside the old mission prepared for a hurricane of enemy troops and return cannon fire.

For almost two weeks, the Texans defended their positions inside the Alamo. Skirmishes took place around the perimeter wall behind the main mission building, but the Texans drove off each assault. Everyone knew, in time, that Santa Anna would launch an all-out attack against the Texans. Desperate for help, Colonel Travis sent out fellow defender, Juan Nepomuceno Seguin, a local wealthy Mexican rancher, and a handful of men to get reinforcements. When halted by Mexican troops, Seguin shouted, in Spanish, "We are countrymen!" which confused the enemy long enough for Seguin and the others to escape amid a hail of Mexican bullets. But before Seguin could return, the Alamo fell.

During the final days of the Mexican siege, Colonel Travis wrote, "I shall never surrender or retreat . . . I am determined to . . . die like a soldier . . . Victory or death!" On March 6, the Mexican army prepared to make their final massive assault against the walls of the beleaguered Alamo. At dawn, Mexican buglers sounded the strains of the deguello, a call used in bullrings to indicate death. The Mexicans intended to take no prisoners.

Throughout several hours of fighting, with Santa Anna ordering four great columns of soldiers to attack the mission defenders, the casualties mounted. Texan riflemen slowed down the massive assault columns, but only for a time. When Mexican troops swarmed in, capturing the Texans' 18-pound cannon, it was all but over.

Houston Leads the Texans to Victory

As hundreds of Mexican soldiers swarmed into the Alamo grounds, the Texans fought desperately. William Travis was shot down defending the outer wall. The remaining Texans were ordered to abandon the perimeter wall and take refuge inside the mission building. They took up defensive positions, but the Mexicans simply outnumbered them. Crockett and his men took up positions in a small room in the lower barracks, but he and his men were soon overwhelmed. Whether Crockett surrendered or fought to his death remains a debated subject even today. Eyewitness accounts vary. Without question, however, he did not survive the battle or its aftermath. (One story states Crockett and his colleagues were taken prisoner and executed on the spot within six feet of General Santa Anna.)

Bowie, lying on his sick bed, was killed as he fired his final shots at the approaching Mexicans. By 6:30 A.M., the final hours of the storming of the Alamo were over. All defenders of the mission were killed. But not without cost to the Mexican army, which had lost over 1,000 men during the 13-day siege. Among the sole survivors inside the Alamo were a Mrs. Dickenson, wife of one of the men, as well as her baby, her Mexican nurse, and a young black man.

When the battle was completed and the Alamo securely in his hands, General Santa Anna gave his assessment of the action at the Alamo to a junior officer, "It was but a small affair." But the defeat of the defenders of the Alamo would soon become a rallying cry for the Texans. Even before the Texans had recovered from the loss, they witnessed another Mexican victory. This time approximately 450 Texans, under the command of Colonel James W. Fannin, surrendered to General Santa Anna in the small community of Goliad, only to be executed under the Mexican general's orders. Cries of "Remember the Alamo!" and "Remember Goliad!" were constantly on the lips of revolutionary Texans everywhere.

Following his victories at the Alamo and Goliad, Santa Anna was certain he had crushed the

Texas rebellion. He set his sights on destroying the rebel government and the small army of Texans led by Sam Houston. Even before the fall of the Alamo, delegates meeting at Washington-on-the-Brazos had altered the nature of the rebellion, declaring Texas independence from Mexico on March 1, 1836. The Texas congress ordered the writing of a republican constitution, and appointed Sam Houston the commander-in-chief of its army.

Too weak to meet Santa Anna's superior numbers, Houston fled ahead of the Mexican forces, looking for a way to attack. Through evasion and delay, he kept Santa Anna's army at a distance, but Houston received much criticism for not hitting Santa Anna's forces head on. By late April, Houston saw his opportunity. Both armies were encamped on April 20, along the banks of the San Jacinto Bayou. That afternoon, just as the Mexican soldiers prepared for their afternoon siesta, Houston and his 800 men army attacked. Houston had kept some of his men up in trees, watching the Mexicans who were unaware of Houston's close presence.

As a ragtag Texas band played "Will You Come to the Bower I have Shaded for You," Houston ordered the surprise assault. The battle lasted approximately 18 minutes. Completely surprised, the Mexican army remained in disarray throughout the skirmish. When the smoke cleared, 630 Mexicans lay dead and 730 were taken prisoners, including President-General Santa Anna, who had tried to disguise himself as a Mexican peasant soldier. In all, the battle resulted in the deaths of eight Texans, with 17 wounded.

The Republic of Texas

With the defeat of the Mexican general, Santa Anna, in the battle of San Jacinto, Sam Houston was able to extract significant concessions from the vanquished president. On May 14, 1836, Santa Anna signed the Treaty of Velasco which granted independence for Texas and established the southern boundary of the Texas republic along the banks of the Rio Grande.

But when the treaty reached the Mexican Congress in Mexico City for ratification, its members refused to recognize the document. Nevertheless, the Americans in Texas saw themselves as the inheritors of a newly freed Republic of Texas.

Four choices now lay before the leaders of an independent Texas. They could remain an independent state, a nation to themselves, serving as a buffer between the United States and Mexico. Second, they could attempt to create an even larger, independent state by campaigning south against Mexico itself. Third, they could attach their new nation by alliances with England and France, providing Texas with European trade access. Lastly, they could make application for annexation as a state of the United States.

Texas chose to apply for statehood. But, surprisingly, they were refused by Congress in 1837. Behind the denial were burning questions and rivalries concerning slavery in the U.S. Many northerners could not abide by the admission of a 14th slave state into the Union, and blocked Texas admission. Congressman John Quincy Adams, a former U.S. president and son of the great patriot leader John Adams, was the leader of the northern opposition. While President Andrew Jackson supported Texas' admission, he could not sweep the tide of opposition. Instead, during his final day as Chief Executive, he offered diplomatic recognition of the Texas Republic.

During the fall of 1836, Texans had held their first elections since the end of the revolution. They cast 5,000 ballots for the popular hero of San Jacinto, Sam Houston, who won a two-year term as the republic's first president. As the political leader of Texas, Houston faced a myriad of problems. Since the Mexican government never officially recognized the republic's legitimacy, there were constant challenges to Houston's authority, as well as domestic issues over land. Indians posed a continual challenge as Texas authorities attempted to control the actions of Comanches, Apaches, and Kiowas.

Many of the Mexicans living in Texas, the Tejanos, would lose their land in the process. American squatters regularly moved them off their legitimately held property, determined to make Texas an American republic. Thousands of Tejanos fled their homes and moved to Mexico. Yet despite the mass migration of Tejanos out of Texas, the Spanish-Mexican influence in Texas would never completely vanish. Even today, cities such as San Antonio have retained their traditional Mexican-American roots.

Throughout the early 1840s, Texas statehood seemed an illusive dream. But during the 1844 presidential campaign, Democratic candidate, James K. Polk, a Tennessee politician, promised to annex Texas as a state if elected. When he was, the future of the Republic took a decisive turn. But outgoing president, John Tyler, took it upon himself to call for the annexation before he left office in the spring of 1845. By December, Texas entered the Union as the 28th state and the 15th slave state (Florida had just become the 14th slave state.)

Review and Write

1. Why did John Quincy Adams attempt to block statehood for Texas?

2. Once Sam Houston's men defeated the Mexican General Santa Anna and his army, the Texans gained their independence. What four courses of action lay before the Texans after they became independent of Mexican rule?

3. When Texas attempted application for American statehood, what U.S. Congressman opposed the inclusion of Texas into the Union and why?

65

Test IV

Part I.

Matching. *Match the answers shown below with the statements given above. Place the letters of the correct answers in the spaces below.*

1. Most assimilated Native American tribe living in Southeast
2. Mystical Shawnee leader who was known as "The Prophet"
3. Name of treaty under which Delaware and Potawatomi surrendered land in Indiana territory
4. American commander during War of 1812 battle of the Thames, fought on October 5, 1813
5. American commander who defeated the Creek Indians in 1814 battle of Horseshoe Bend
6. Act allowing the purchase of 80 acres of government land at $1.25 per acre
7. Portion of Southeast which extends from Gulf of Florida to lower Mississippi River
8. Shawnee warrior who rallied and unified Ohio tribes against white influences
9. Chief Justice of U.S. Supreme Court who rendered *Cherokee Nation v. Georgia* decision
10. Seminole chief who resisted removal by U.S. Army from Southeast
11. Route taken by Cherokees from Tennessee and Georgia homelands to Oklahoma reserve
12. Plantation owner who hosted Eli Whitney when he invented the cotton gin

A. Fort Wayne	B. Land Act of 1820	C. John Marshall	D. Catherine Greene
E. Tenskwatawa	F. Andrew Jackson	G. Cherokees	H. Trail of Tears
I. Tecumseh	J. William Harrison	K. Gulf Plains	L. Osceola

1. ____ 2. ____ 3. ____ 4. ____ 5. ____ 6. ____ 7. ____ 8. ____ 9. ____ 10. ____ 11. ____ 12. ____

Part II.

Matching. *Match the answers shown below with the statements given above. Place the letters of the correct answers in the spaces below.*

1. British outpost for western fur trade located on the lower Columbia River
2. Site of second Texas massacre of James Fannin's 450 Texans
3. Annual site for mountain man gathering where furs were sold and supplies purchased
4. American newspaperman who coined the term "Manifest Destiny"
5. Missourian who received one of first land grants from Mexican government for Texas land
6. American empresario who attempted a revolution against Mexico to establish Fredonia
7. Became Mexican president after he came to power by military force in 1833
8. Site of the Alamo
9. American commander of the Alamo during the famous 1836 siege
10. Mexican bugle call sounded before final assault against the Alamo defenders
11. Spanish center for fur trade, located just 100 miles north of Santa Fe
12. 1844 presidential candidate who campaigned in support of annexation of Texas as U.S. state

A. rendezvous	B. Hayden Edwards	C. William Travis	D. James K. Polk
E. Taos	F. San Antonio de Bexar	G. Stephen Austin	H. Goliad
I. Fort Vancouver	J. John O'Sullivan	K. Santa Anna	L. deguello

1. ____ 2. ____ 3. ____ 4. ____ 5. ____ 6. ____ 7. ____ 8. ____ 9. ____ 10. ____ 11. ____ 12. ____

The Oregon Country

With each passing decade of the 19th century, Americans were taking an interest in other parts of the Far West. Although the Oregon Country (which included modern-day Washington, Oregon, and Idaho) had been claimed for decades by the British, as well as the Russians and Spanish, more and more Americans were taking a serious look in the direction of Oregon.

But, despite American interest, the non-Indian nation with the deepest roots in the Oregon Country in the early 1800s was Great Britain. British fur agents had arrived along the Columbia River during the 1700s, and the Hudson Bay Company had consolidated the British presence by establishing Fort Vancouver on the Columbia River. Prior to 1800, few Americans had even seen Oregon. One, an American sea captain named Robert Gray, had reached the mouth of the Columbia during the early 1790s and claimed the region for the United States.

The American explorers Lewis and Clark reached Oregon during their expedition in 1805-06, giving further legitimacy to an American claim to the region. A permanent American outpost was established in 1811 by American fur entrepreneur John Jacob Astor, who opened his trading fort, Astoria, on the opposite side of the Columbia from British Fort Vancouver.

For years, the British and the Americans could not agree even on the boundaries of Oregon, much less the issue of who "owned" the region. In 1818, the two nations agreed to jointly occupy it, giving citizens from both nations the right to trade and establish farms and outposts. The treaty was renewed in 1827.

In the 1830s, American missionaries trekked out to Oregon, settling in the fertile Willamette Valley. Already American mountain men had established a wagon route across the West from Missouri to Oregon. The trail first saw wagons in 1830, under the ownership of the Rocky Mountain Fur Company. That first group of wagons was carrying trade goods to the local mountain man rendezvous. Among the missionaries to Oregon were Presbyterian minister Marcus Whitman and his wife, Narcissa, who established a mission for the Cayuse Indians living near Walla Walla, Washington, near an outpost of the Hudson's Bay Company.

In just a few years, other migrants from America, pioneers looking for cheap, fertile, land, followed, using the Oregon Trail as their primary road across the Far West. The first overland wagon trains to use the trail did so in 1841 under the leadership of a Missourian named John Bidwell. Although 500 people signed on for the trail trek, only about 70 actually went. Of that number, about half arrived in Oregon, while the other half chose to travel to California.

Thousands of pioneers followed. By 1844, the Democratic presidential candidate, James K. Polk, campaigned on two promises—that he would annex Texas to the Union, and that he would bring Oregon into the United States. Polk even claimed that the Oregon Country included territory as far north as the line of latitude 54 degrees, 40 minutes, which would include much of modern-day British Columbia. After his election, Polk was able to negotiate with the British and gain a treaty recognizing a line further south as the boundary between American territory and British claims. The 49th parallel was fixed, making Oregon—the land including today's states of Oregon, Washington, and Idaho—part of the United States.

Already, Americans were living there, hundreds of them, hearty pioneers who had followed the rugged western route known as the Oregon Trail.

Wagons on the Oregon Trail

Once missionary women, such as Narcissa Whitman, proved that the Oregon Trail trek was not too difficult an experience for females, the trail became widely used as farm families moved west to both the Oregon Country and California.

Following Bidwell's 1841 wagon train, which included men, women, and children, emigration on the trail increased in numbers. In 1842, 200 Americans used the trail to travel to the West. The next year, a Great Migration of over 1,000 people pushed their way across the Great Plains and the mountains of the Far West, traveling in 120 wagons. Many of those traveling the trail that year were led by missionary Marcus Whitman.

For the next thirty years, hundreds of thousands of Americans and others would use the Oregon Trail as their highway to the West. This 2,000 mile long wagon route stretched across grasslands in Nebraska, the mountains of Wyoming, and along western flowing rivers. Originating from Independence, Missouri, to the Willamette Valley in Oregon, it was a bumpy, difficult, exhausting, and dangerous six-month trip for both people and their draft animals. Many of the earlier wagon trains were ill-prepared and ill-equipped to complete the arduous journey. The route was so challenging, it required the development of a special wagon.

For decades, pioneers and farmers had relied on the great workhorse wagon of the eastern United States, the Conestoga wagon. Such wagons were strong and durable, but too heavy for much use on the western trails. Conestogas were huge, boat-shaped wagons unsuitable for uneven landscapes, mountain passes, and for fording swollen mountain rivers and streams. A smaller wagon, but one just as sturdy, was needed.

The typical western wagon would be reduced in size, the wagon box measuring about 10 feet long, by 4 feet wide, by 2 feet deep, cut out of ash wood. The various wheel parts were made from elm, Osage orange, oak, hickory, ash or beech. The wagon, when empty, weighed about 1,000 pounds, and was capable of hauling between 1,000 and 1,500 pounds of well-packed household goods. Like the Conestoga, the western wagon featured wooden hoops, covered with a white canvas, allowing about 5 feet of headroom. The canvas covering was waterproofed with a treatment of linseed oil.

To provide for additional storage, pioneers often sewed pockets on the insides of their coverings to hold smaller everyday items. To help prepare the common "prairie schooner" for western use, the

wagon box was caulked, making it watertight. Often, prairie schooners featured a toolbox on one side and a 40-gallon water barrel on the other.

While the typical Conestoga wagon back east might be pulled by horses, the western wagons needed an even more dependable stock. For that reason, pioneers used six oxen, yoked in pairs. Six mules could also do the job, as even four oxen might. In fact, four were often utilized, with an additional pair rotated in to relieve the others. Oxen were also used in the West for other duties. Oxen were inexpensive to purchase and would feed on prairie grass. A typical ox cost about $50, while a mule might run $90. They would not run away and thieves, including Indians, would not usually steal them.

Oxen were not noted for their speed, just their endurance. Oxen could pull a fully-loaded wagon at a rate of about two miles an hour over flat country. On a typical day's travel on the Oregon Trail, a wagon train might cover about 15 miles, with 20 miles covered on an extraordinary day.

Preparing for the Way West

In reality, no day of travel on the Oregon Trail was typical. Each held its own challenges, dreams, and even terrors. Life on the trail was fraught with hardship, as pioneers pressed on daily with high hopes.

The ride on a covered wagon was, in a word, rough. Rarely did such wagons have springs to soften the ride, or even brakes to stop the wagon in an emergency. Even steering was difficult. The problem was in the physics of the covered wagon. When turning, the outside rear wheel turned at the same speed as the inner one even though it was covering more ground, resulting in the outer wheel sliding or skidding throughout the entire turn, depending on the speed of the wagon.

Pioneer families traveling west had to plan ahead. Such planning would make the trip either bearable or miserable. A lack of planning might result in death. Food was an important part of preparing for the trail. A typical family purchased food to last six months, including the following:

150 pounds of flour
40 pounds of sugar
40 pounds of coffee
40 pounds of smoked bacon
25 pounds of salt
5 pounds of baking soda
30-40 pounds of dried fruit

Travelers packed away such "necessities" as yeast for baking, vinegar, molasses, even chocolate. Other foods would be included, depending on the tastes of the family. A pioneer larder might include rice, cornmeal, hardtack, dried beans, and dried beef. Eggs could be packed and protected when placed separately in barrels of cornmeal or flour. Additional meat was provided by hunting along the route. Coffee was the most popular drink on the trail, and even children consumed it. Pioneers boiled it hearty and black to take the edge off western water which was sometimes bitter, due to the alkali content. (Some horses who might refuse to drink western water would drink coffee.)

Fresh dairy products on the trail were difficult to come by. Cows were taken along and milked daily. Leftover milk each morning might be placed in a watertight pail and suspended from the back of the wagon. A day's jolting and bumping on the trail produced butter.

Cooking on the trail was difficult business. Every day, the women cooked on open fires. Firewood was sometimes scarce, so women and children spent time each day while crossing the Great Plains picking up dried pieces of buffalo dung, called "buffalo chips," that could be burned for fuel. Women also brought along Dutch ovens, sheet-iron stoves of simple, light design, which could be used to bake bread and other foods. An additional problem with trail cooking were the altitudes, where even boiling water was nearly impossible.

Another important aspect of planning before setting out on the Oregon Trail was locating a skilled guide. Only men of experience could be relied on for the daily decisions that would help frontier families complete the western trek. Also, the would-be pioneers needed to know what routes were the best to follow and which promised more than they could deliver. Several different trail guides were published—one of the first in 1831 by Hall Jackson Kelley. Another, entitled *The Emigrants' Guide to Oregon and California* was written in 1842 by Lansford W. Hastings, who first led pioneers west on the Oregon Trail.

Once all the planning was completed, and pioneers attached themselves to various wagon trains, they readied for the high adventure and challenge that lay ahead.

Review and Write

How did the pioneers on the Oregon Trail use the natural elements they found on the trail to their advantage?

Marking the Oregon Trail

Embarking on the 2000-mile long trail to Oregon required great courage, stamina, and strength for all those who sought a better life in the West. Taking the trail to either Oregon Country or California meant leaving extended family members behind, loved ones the pioneers would likely never see again.

Wagon trains left from Independence, Missouri, the great gathering place on the trail. Most left in April, following the spring thaws of the western rivers. Also, a spring departure would mean the prairie grasses of Kansas and Nebraska would be tall and available in abundance to feed the livestock.

Leaving from Independence, the typical train followed the old, nearly abandoned route of the Santa Fe Trail for two days, generally headed straight west. Then, about 40 miles out from Independence, the wagon train reached a simple, wooden sign pointing toward the north, requiring a right hand turn. Although still nearly 2000 miles from their destination, the sign read, "To Oregon."

Travel was slow, methodical, even monotonous while crossing the relative flatlands of Kansas and Nebraska. About four weeks out from Independence, the wagon train reached Fort Kearney, situated on the south bank of the Platte River. By then, the pioneer party had covered 400 miles since leaving Missouri and had crossed rivers, but the shallow Platte River was difficult given its soft and shifting bottom.

The portion of the trail through Nebraska was an endless stretch of prairie grass. More miles of the trail crossed modern-day Nebraska than any other state. Pioneers, once arriving in the western portion of the territory, watched for massive rock formations to indicate their progress. Natural outcroppings, such as Court House Rock, Chimney Rock, and Scott's Bluff, located in the Nebraska panhandle, were welcome sites. Once they crossed over into modern-day Wyoming, the train reached Fort Laramie, indicating the party had covered one-third of the trail's length.

A stop at Fort Laramie provided a break from the usual trail experience. Owned by the American Fur Company (Laramie did not become a U.S. Army post until 1849), pioneers could get their wagons repaired, buy needed supplies, and talk with others at the fort about the trail ahead.

Once back on the trail, the pioneers followed the North Platte and Sweetwater Rivers, as they approached the foothills of the Rockies. Beyond Fort Laramie, the train arrived near Register Cliff, where many carved their names, recording their passage along the western route. Others signed in at Independence Rock, named for the fact that a train making good progress would arrive there by the 4th of July.

Upon reaching the Rockies, the wagon train passed over the Continental Divide at South Pass, a wide natural break in the mountains. Some pioneers continued southwest toward California, following the trail north of the Great Salt Lake to the Humboldt River, then through the Sierra Nevadas to California.

Continuing on, the wagon train reached Soda Springs, Idaho. By now, the party had passed the 1000-mile point. Pioneers drank here from the bubbly mineral waters. The next stop was Fort Hall, where the train would follow the Snake River. This leg of the trip was extremely difficult as the trail was cut by rivers, requiring wagons to follow narrow cliff trails, and other obstacles. Arriving at the Snake River, the pioneers continued on to Fort Boise, then to Walla Walla mission. With the greater challenges behind them, the emigrants were soon in the Willamette Valley.

Review and Write

1. What was the significance of reaching Fort Laramie and what advantages did the fort offer the trail's pioneers?

2. Once pioneers passed through the continental Divide at South Pass, the trail became two trails. Explain.

Days on the Wagon Trains West

For nearly 200 days, pioneers endured an experience of hardship and challenge on the Oregon Trail. While each day might include disappointments, tiring labor, and challenge, many of those who completed the journey often spoke of it in their later years as the greatest adventure of their lives. Each day might feature new vistas, grand mountain scenery, or the beauty of a herd of buffalo, elk, antelope, or deer. An occasional Indian might ride by, more curious than menacing, watching these travelers cross his land.

But most days were filled with a drudgery similar to the previous day's. Wagon trains typically settled into a regular schedule of daily events, a structure of routine designed to make something predictable about a day which might include a hail storm, a wagon accident, or even a tragic death at the hands of an unexplained illness.

Most days began at 4 A.M. when the night guards fired their rifles, awakening the sleeping pioneers. Fires from the night before were rekindled, as families tumbled out of bedrolls, dressing for the rigors ahead. The men and boys rounded up the train's livestock. Most of the animals had remained together through the night as a protection against wolves.

By 5 A.M., the animals were to be harnessed or yoked. A quick breakfast, which might include bacon and a bread, such as a biscuit or a pancake they called slam-johns, was downed, and the camp taken down. Within two hours, the train was formed up, the wagons stretching behind one another in single file. Often, a wagon train might extend three-quarters of a mile from the lead wagon to the end. Wagons were regularly rotated so that everyone had a chance to take the lead on occasion.

As the wagon train slowly progressed across the prairie, the day became a regular routine. There could be a sameness to the landscape, especially across the Plains. Most pioneers chose to walk, if they could, since riding on a wagon could be a jaw-jolting experience. Children ran and played or gathered buffalo chips. Sometimes they threw them, sailing the animal waste like Frisbees. Some children herded animals, including cows and goats. For many of them, this was an exciting time, a break from the endless chores that had preoccupied their days on the farm.

After four hours of travel—having covered usually no more distance than ten miles—the wagons were halted for the day's nooning. It was lunchtime, and the women would serve a cold meal, not bothering to light a fire. If a stream ran nearby, women might wash some clothing. The animals were let out to feed and the men checked their equipment, including harnesses, ox hooves, wagon wheels, and axles. Scouts from up ahead reported back on what the afternoon might bring to the pioneer party.

By 2 P.M., the train was in motion again, moving through the longest portion of the day. Some wagon trains kept on the move even after dark, remaining on the trail until 10 P.M., especially during a full moon. But typically, a train might stop around 6 P.M. to make camp.

As the wagon train halted for the evening, fires were lit, meals cooked, and animals unharnessed. Often the wagons were drawn up in a circle and chained together. If the train included enough wagons, they divided up into eight-wagon units, each called a mess. The evening meal was the heaviest of the day, and might include stew, buffalo steak, or stewed prairie chicken. After dinner, the pioneers might listen to fiddle music, read their Bibles, and complete their chores. Only then, did they crawl wearily off to sleep having moved 15 miles closer to Oregon that day.

Death on the Trail

In addition to the daily challenges afforded by travel along the Oregon Trail, there was always the possibility of death. The trail disguised a dozen ways to die, from contracting a disease from another member of the party, to a wagon accident, to a gunshot wound, to drowning during one of the many river crossings.

Disease was a constant threat and fear. It struck migrants of all ages and once a contagious illness broke out, it often ran through the entire wagon train like wildfire. One of the common diseases of the era was dysentery. Pioneers called it the relax disease, and it was caused by poor sanitation. With no indoor plumbing, streams were often fouled by human waste, causing people to become sick. Dysentery did not always kill, but it caused its victims to suffer greatly, as the illness included repeated bouts of diarrhea.

But the most dreaded disease of the trail was cholera, a gastrointestinal illness, which typically killed very quickly, in a matter of days. Some pioneers who contracted the disease in the morning were dead before the day ended. With cholera, the victim dies through dehydration caused by vomiting and diarrhea.

Carried by bacteria, cholera had been introduced to the United States from Asia and had spread during the 1830s and 40s through America's urban centers. Some of the major outbreaks in cities such as Philadelphia or New York had encouraged some Americans to leave and take to the trail to escape the deadly virus. In the process, they inadvertently brought the disease with them. A victim of cholera was typically buried hastily to avoid further contamination. Trail graves were either dug deeply or were covered over with heavy rocks to keep wolves from digging up the corpses and mutilating them.

Accidents were around every turn on the Oregon Trail. Since most pioneers did not know how to swim, drowning was commonplace during river crossings. Occasionally, a wagon might slip off a mountain trail, killing someone inside. Children might fall off the wagon and be crushed under the slowly moving, but heavy wheels.

Gunshot wounds were also common, but not from encountering robbers or Indians. Instead, most gunshot victims accidentally shot themselves. Many pioneers brought no real experience with firearms with them on the trail. A common mishap was made when men stuck handguns in their belts, causing them to go off. Such wounds could be fatal, or, at least, embarrassing.

Others died from buffalo stampedes, from being poisoned by alkali water, from suffering heart attacks and strokes from overexertion, or from appendicitis. Modern historians estimate that the death toll on the Oregon Trail was about 34,000 people, or nearly one out of every ten pioneers. This figure would account for 17 deaths for each mile of the 2,000-mile-long trail.

An infrequent cause of death on the Oregon Trail was murder at the hands of Indians. Despite what Hollywood movies have portrayed over the past 60 years, Indian attacks against wagon trains were extremely rare. For example, during the 1840s and '50s, approximately 250,000 people traveled the Oregon Trail, or the Big Medicine Path, as Native Americans called it. Of that number, only about 362 pioneers died from Indian attack. By comparison, approximately 425 Indians were killed by pioneers.

Review and Write

How did pioneers on the Oregon Trail die?

The Mormons Move West

As thousands travelled the Oregon Trail west during the 1840s, one unique group of pioneers was a religious sect called the Church of Jesus Christ of Latter-Day Saints. Popularly, they were known as the Mormons.

This sect was founded in 1827, by a New Yorker named Joseph Smith, who claimed to have been visited by an angel named Moroni, son of the prophet, Mormon. The angel, according to Smith, led him to a set of golden plates and provided him with a pair of special glasses which allowed Smith to translate the texts into English. The plates served as the source for a book by Smith titled, The Book of Mormon.

According to the book, two lost tribes of Israel migrated from the ancient world to North America. The evil tribe, the Indians, triumphed over the good tribe, the Nephites. Only two Nephites survived, Mormon and Moroni. They wrote their book on the gold plates and buried them in upstate New York, around A.D. 400.

In time, the gold plates discovered by Joseph Smith disappeared, but *The Book of Mormon* became the basis for a new Christian religion, Mormonism, with Joseph Smith as its leader. Many people in the East were converted, and the Church of Jesus Christ of Latter-Day Saints was established.

As a religious group, the Mormons separated themselves from everyone else, those they called Gentiles, and became known for their clannishness and mysterious religious ways. Rumors circulated that the Mormons were secretly practicing polygamy, the practice of having multiple wives.

Smith believed his goal as prophet was to established a New Zion in the West. To that end, he moved his followers to Ohio, then to Independence, Missouri, where they were driven out by the locals who mistrusted the close-knit cult. Ultimately, the governor of Missouri ordered all Mormons to leave his state. By 1839, Smith had established his people in Nauvoo, Illinois, on the Mississippi River, where they flourished, building a great temple and an industrious community of believers. Rumors of

polygamy were discovered to be true, and popular sentiment again turned against them. (The theology behind Mormon polygamy was that single women could not be saved, so it was a man's duty to marry as many as he could.) In time, Joseph Smith and his brother were arrested for treason (the Mormons voted as a block and could manipulate local laws in their favor). A mob stormed the jail in Carthage, and killed the Smith brothers.

A new leader emerged among the Mormons' ranks. A tall, Vermont carpenter named Brigham Young became the president of the sect and determined that his people should move into the Far West to avoid further persecution by Gentiles. The entire Nauvoo community turned to wagon making, even building them in their Temple.

A great migration of Mormons west followed. In February 1846, they crossed the frozen Mississippi River and encamped in Iowa. By spring, 16,000 Mormons were assembled. They slowly moved across Iowa, a caravan of 400 wagons, and encamped through the winter of 1846–47, along the Missouri River, near Omaha, where local Indians, including the Potawatomi and the Omaha, provided them with some food.

By spring of 1847, Brigham Young set out along the Oregon Trail with 73 wagons of Mormons. They crossed the plains, entered South Pass, and arrived at Fort Bridger by mid-June. Then, uncertain of where they intended to reestablish themselves, Young directed his followers off the main trail and headed south toward the Great Salt Lake. Here, the Mormons established their settlement.

Review and Write

1. Describe the founding of the Church of Jesus Christ of Latter-Day Saints. What was Joseph Smith's role and why did the group come to be known popularly as the Mormons?

2. Under what circumstance did Brigham Young take the reins of leadership of the Mormon faith?

Texas Dispute Leads to War

Throughout much of the 19th century, America's drive to dominate the vast open lands of the Trans-Mississippi West, as well as the Far West, seemed to know no limits. During the 1840s, America would go to war with Mexico to acquire additional territory that the Mexican government had not intended to surrender. The Mexican War was a conflict of America's making.

The primary antagonist was President James K. Polk, who was elected in 1844, on a platform that promised the annexation of both the Oregon Country and Texas. Texas became a state in 1845, and Polk successfully negotiated for Oregon under an 1846 treaty. But as an expansionist president, he intended to acquire even more territory.

During the spring of 1846, relations between Mexico and the U.S. deteriorated dramatically. There was controversy over the American acquisition of Oregon and the annexation of Texas as an American state. When the United States claimed Texas to include the land north of the Rio Grande, the Mexicans were furious. The Mexican government had never recognized the Rio Grande, but rather the Nueces River, as the boundary of the Republic of Texas.

By looking at the maps of the day, the Mexicans were correct in designating the Nueces as the actual border river of Texas. General Santa Anna had accepted the Rio Grande as the border in the Treaty of Velasco, but that treaty was never ratified by the Mexican Congress. Polk did not intend to listen to the Mexicans and their rightful claims.

In June of 1845, just months after the annexation of Texas, President Polk sent General Zachary Taylor into Texas where, by October, Taylor led American forces to the northern bank of the Rio Grande as a direct challenge to Mexican forces. By doing so, Polk intended to stir up a war. At the same time he sent Taylor to the Rio Grande, Polk secretly dispatched U.S. Naval vessels to Mexican-controlled California. Polk also sent instructions to the American envoy in Monterey, Thomas Larkin, that the U.S. would welcome a revolt of Californians against the Mexican government.

On another front, Polk sent an American negotiator to Mexico City to offer to buy the lands from California to Texas for $25 million. If that failed, the representative was to offer to pay to establish the Rio Grande as the Texas border. But envoy John Slidell was not even given an audience with Mexican officials, who were not interested in any such offer from the United States.

An angry Polk responded to the Mexican rebuff by ordering General Taylor and his men to cross the Nueces and take up positions along the banks of the Rio Grande in defiance of the Mexicans. In April 1846, Mexican troops, in the battle of Palo Alto, attacked the American military presence, prompting Polk to appeal to Congress for a declaration of war.

In his speech, Polk attempted to stir animosity against the Mexicans by stating, "Mexico has passed the boundary of the United States, has invaded our territory, and shed American blood upon American soil . . . War exists, and notwithstanding all our efforts to avoid it, exists by the act of Mexico herself." Polk's words dramatically stretched the truth. Such lies caused Congress to vote in favor of war with Mexico on May 13, 1846.

As the Mexican-American War began, it bitterly divided the United States. Whig leaders challenged Democrat Polk's intentions and accused him of fabricating events to force a war on Mexico. The Massachusetts state legislature voted a resolution condemning Polk's actions, and the Transcendental writer, Henry David Thoreau, refused to pay his taxes in support of such a shameful war, causing him to be arrested and to spend one night in jail.

Review and Write

1. What issue caused relations between Mexico and the United States to deteriorate by the spring of 1846?

2. After Texas became a state, what did Polk do to provoke a war against Mexico?

The Mexican-American War

As the Mexican-American War commenced, President Polk was soon highly criticized. Whig detractors referred to the conflict as "Mr. Polk's War." In some respects, such a name for the war was an accurate one. Polk, although he had little military experience, used his role as Commander-in-Chief to establish strategy and military goals for the war. A micro-manager during the conflict, Polk repeatedly coordinated political goals and military goals, giving greater role to the nation's Chief Executive than was held previously.

Once again, President Polk sent General Taylor south, this time deeper into Mexican territory. In addition, the president sent Colonel Stephen Kearney into New Mexico and California, where U.S. military troops were to occupy northern Mexican cities, such as Palo Alto and Monterrey. Both towns were captured by Americans in May and September 1846, respectively.

Colonel Kearney arrived in Santa Fe, New Mexico, following a 900-mile march, where nearly the entire local population surrendered peacefully. Kearney marched on to California where he took control with the help of American naval forces and a handful of tenacious, American revolutionaries living in California and led by Army explorer John C. Fremont.

With American victories in both California and New Mexico, Polk anticipated the Mexican government would be prepared to sue for peace, and write terms of surrender. But the Mexicans did no such thing. This forced Polk to dispatch General Taylor south. Taylor engaged a Mexican army under the command of General Santa Anna at Buena Vista, near Monterrey, Mexico, in February 1847. But Santa Anna was unable to defeat the tenacious American commander. Within weeks, another American army, under the command of General Winfield Scott landed U.S. troops in the Mexican city of Veracruz, along the Gulf Coast. These two victories helped to stir the hearts of Americans everywhere.

General Scott continued his march across Mexico, toward the capital city, Mexico City. Scott's advance was slow, requiring six months of hard fighting, as Scott faced a constant, daily challenge of guerrilla tactics. American casualties ran high, as Scott's army moved further into the Mexican interior. But U.S. army personnel regularly carried out atrocities against the citizens of Mexico, including murder and rape. By September 1847, Scott's forces arrived in the Mexican capital and occupied the city, effectively ending the military action of the war.

Almost immediately, an American negotiator, Nicholas Trist, who had moved along with Scott's army, began negotiating with the Mexicans for terms of peace. The result was the Treaty of Guadalupe Hidalgo, signed on February 2, 1848. Under the agreement, a defeated Mexico surrendered control of its northern lands, including modern-day California, Arizona, Utah, Nevada, and a portion of southern Colorado. In exchange for this vast land grab, Trist promised the United States would pay Mexico $15 million, plus an additional $2 million in claims against Mexico.

Ironically, Trist's treaty did not satisfy President Polk, who was determined to take the opportunity to seize all of Mexico. But political pressure exerted on Polk by northern Whigs and southerners opposed to making Mexicans citizens of the U.S., forced him to accept the treaty.

By 1853, the government negotiated an additional treaty with Mexico, paying $10 million for the southern portions of Arizona and New Mexico, land totaling additional 30,000 square miles. America's greed for land continued without limits.

The Bear Flag Revolt

Before the Mexican War, which delivered California into the hands of the U.S. government, the great coastal region was home to dozens of small tribes of Native Americans (approximately 50,000 residents), and 7000 Californios, Spanish-speaking Mexicans, many of whom descended from families that had lived in California since the late 1700s. But in just a few years, by 1850, California would become a state in the American Union. This great change occurred when gold was discovered in the rivers west of the Sierra Nevadas.

The Americans who rushed to California after the 1848 discovery of gold were not the first to arrive in this region. Following Mexico's independence from Spain in 1821, California's trade policy was open to other nations. California's closest trading partner was Russia, until 1832, when the Russians moved out of California's markets and established trade relations with the Hudson's Bay Company in the Pacific Northwest.

With the trade gap caused by the Russians needing filling, the Americans wasted little time. One of the first trade connections between Americans and Californios was a Swiss immigrant who had become a Mexican citizen, Johann Augustus Sutter. Sutter owned a ranch in the Sacramento Valley where he had erected Sutter's Fort, a self-sufficient outpost for his cattle ranch. As more and more Americans travelled the Oregon Trail in the 1840s, some of them migrated to California and found support from Sutter. Since these Americans were intent on California becoming their territory, Sutter played an important part in providing them security and supplies.

The first serious American challenge to Mexican authority in California took place in June of 1846, when a band of Americans joined forces at Sonoma (north of present-day San Francisco), calling for independence from Mexico. They created an emblem for their revolution, a flag featuring an image of a bear, giving the insurrection the name of Bear Flag Revolt.

One of the revolt's leaders was an American

explorer and army officer, John C. Fremont. Fremont was on an exploring expedition in California when he received orders from President James K. Polk and Secretary of State James Buchanan to arrange with the American envoy to Monterey, Thomas O. Larkin, for a local rebellion against the Mexican government. To an extent, the fact that so many Californio landowners, including Colonel Mariano Vallejo (vi-YAY-ho), were dissatisfied with Mexican rule simply helped Fremont in his revolutionary efforts.

But Fremont's Bear Flag Revolt, even after establishing the California Bear Flag Republic, lost its purpose when the Mexican War resulted in the acquisition of California from Mexico. Under the 1848 Treaty of Guadalupe Hidalgo, the Southwest, from California to Texas, became American territory.

Polk's dream of an American-controlled California was based in the potential of using the great natural harbors of San Diego and San Francisco as the springboards for extensive Pacific trade with Asia. But that dream was interrupted in 1849, with the discovery of gold in northern California, on the property of Johann Sutter.

The initial discovery was made by a carpenter-employee of Sutter's named James Marshall who was building a tailrace for a mill on Sutter's property. Although Marshall and Sutter attempted to keep the discovery quiet, news soon leaked out. Once gold was known to exist, the history of California would never be the same.

The California Gold Rush

Almost an entire year passed from the discovery of gold at Sutter's Mill in January of 1848, until a stampede of gold-seekers descended on California in 1849. As early as the fall of 1848, rumors of gold in California were beginning to circulate as far away as the East Coast. The rumors soon became fact, however, when an army courier brought a tea caddy to Washington, D.C. filled with gold dust and small nuggets. From that moment, the race to California and its riches was on.

Thousands of people, mostly men, dropped everything and headed west. Some left jobs, farms, even families, drawn by the lure of quick riches in California. They came throughout the year 1849, earning the nickname of "Forty-Niners." But where did they come from specifically? The greatest majority of the Forty-Niners—four out of five— were Americans. They came from every corner of America, including every state and territory. In addition, about 13 percent of these "miners" came from Mexico and Latin America. Another 7 percent came from Europe.

The Chinese were one of the largest ethnic groups to flood into California. They arrived in 1849 and 1850, several hundred thousand strong. In 1852, 20,000 arrived in San Francisco alone. Most did not intend to remain for long—just long enough to strike it rich and then return to their homeland. But because many did not achieve great wealth, they remained in the West, establishing businesses, and helping to build the first Transcontinental Railroad.

The gathering point for would-be California prospectors was San Francisco harbor. Home to fewer than 1,000 residents in early 1848, San Francisco became an expanding city of 35,000 by 1850. While nearly everyone came to California to find wealth in the gold mining camps, some ingenious entrepreneurs sought to cash in on the gold rush in other ways. Typically, those who offered a unique service to the miners reaped high profits for their labor. Those who went to California to provide supplies, or clothing, shoes, or other necessities to the miners were often handsomely rewarded with high profits. The German Jewish immigrant, Levi Strauss, brought a bolt of canvas to the gold camps and created a unique pair of pants, fastened together with copper rivets for the hard-working miners. These pants would become the first Levi jeans.

San Francisco became a boom town filled with thousands of miners, prospectors, entrepreneurs, and card sharks. Life became expensive as high inflation developed in the gold camps, driven by the ready availability of gold.

But life in the mining camps themselves could be exciting, dangerous, disappointing and even monotonous. Most of the mining camps were established east of Sutter's Mill and west of the Sierra Nevadas, along the icy, mountainous rivers of the region. Camps with names such as Placerville, Angels Camp, Whiskey Bar, Poker Flat, and Git-Up-and-Git dotted the lands around the American River and its tributaries. Living in the "the diggings" could be monotonous, disappointing, and unhealthy.

Few prospectors struck it rich. Days were spent squatting in cold mountain streams, panning for the shiny metal, and many a miner went broke, drifting off to other gold strikes across the West with the passing of the years. But enough of them stayed, swelling California's population to 100,000, making statehood possible by 1850.

Review and Write

1. How did the discovery of gold alter the history of California dramatically?

2. Who were the "Forty-Niners" and where did they come from?

3. The gold rush encouraged tens of thousands to try their luck at mining but many did not find gold. What difficulties did they face instead?

Mining Across the West

Following the discovery of gold in California and the rush of hopeful miners in search of natural treasure, additional gold and silver strikes occurred across the frontier throughout the remainder of the 19th century. Just as the discovery of gold and silver led to the rapid development of California (nearly 225,000 people lived there by 1852), soon other sites witnessed their own gold rushes.

In 1858, prospectors flooded to the Pike's Peak region of modern-day Colorado after gold was discovered there. Ramshackle mining camps and towns sprang up such as Denver, Pueblo, and Boulder. By 1859, 100,000 prospectors and others had taken up residence. But the boom did not last. Typically, in the early days of a gold rush, the miners removed the surface gold, through panning and other forms of placer mining, or water-washed prospecting. The remaining metals, buried deep underground, required expensive machinery. Mining companies with investment capital to purchase such equipment sprang up.

That same year, a great strike was made along the western border between California and Nevada. Through the discovery of the Comstock Lode, a series of mines were constructed. (The miner after whom the discovery was named sold his stake in the strike for $11,000 and two mules.) Over the next 30 years, those mines extracted a modern-day equivalent of billions of dollars of gold and silver. Virginia City was established as an early Nevada mining town.

Other strikes sent western miners scurrying in every direction. In the late 1850s, a small strike was made in eastern Washington. Miners found gold along the Snake and Salmon rivers in Idaho, where they established Boise, Silver City, and other mining communities. By 1861, 30,000 new inhabitants were living in Idaho.

Additional strikes were made in Montana, where gold-seekers founded Last Chance Gulch, later known as Helena. By 1863, Idaho had enough people to apply for territorial status, and Montana followed suit by the next year.

When gold was discovered in the Dakota Territory in 1874, miners were soon tramping across Indian reserves set aside by the government for the Lakota peoples, causing an Indian war. Other Native American conflicts occurred due to the intrusion of miners onto Indian lands.

While most surface prospectors never became rich, there were great profits possible for those mining companies who invested in the West. Mines were dug deep underground to depths of nearly one mile, with horizontal tunnels established off of main vertical shafts. Massive equipment was installed at such corporate-operated mines to process and crush ore and extract the precious metals. Underground miners relied on the latest equipment, typically steam-powered, including diamond-tipped rotary drills.

Working underground in such mines was difficult and dangerous work. Miners lived in a hellish world of half-lit darkness, dust, and heat. A miner's drill might break through a pocket of heated water, scalding the worker to death. Miners developed lung problems from breathing the dusty mine air. Hardrock mining proved to be such hazardous work that, during the 1870s, one out of every 30 miners became disabled, and one of every 80 died on the job.

While such extensive mining provided an abundance of gold and silver, some of which worked its way into the American economy, the value of western mining was that it encouraged the building of western communities, helping to establish permanent occupation of the West by non-Indians.

Western Transportation Systems

With the number of western gold and silver strikes taking place during the 1850s, '60s, and '70s, along with the pioneer settlement of Oregon, and the establishment of statehood for California in 1850, the demand for safe, fast, and economical transportation and mail delivery grew louder and louder. Many of the mining towns of the West were established in remote corners, with a need to remain connected to the outside world. When corporate mines were opened, the necessity of good roads and transportation systems was even more important.

Freight wagons became the lifeblood for the mining camps and the mining companies that replaced them. One of the most important freighting companies was developed in 1853, by William B. Waddell and William H. Russell, both veterans of the Santa Fe trade. By 1858, their company employed 4,000 teamsters operating 3,500 freight wagons pulled by 40,000 oxen.

In 1858, the first stagecoach line across the west was opened for business. It was popularly known as the Butterfield Overland Express (named for former stagecoach driver turned investor, John Butterfield), and its route ran 2,000 miles across the West, from St. Louis to Sacramento. The Butterfield route was a southern trail, extending through Texas, New Mexico, and Arizona. A trip by stagecoach took 24 days, certainly shorter than a wagon trip over the Oregon Trail or around South America by sea. But stagecoaching was difficult. The primitive roads were excruciating. When writer Mark Twain traveled west, he referred to his stagecoach as a "cradle on wheels." Stagecoaches were dusty, vulnerable to Indian attack, and the stage station food was typically miserable, sometimes including condemned Army bacon.

While stagecoaches delivered the mail across the West, many people wanted an even faster service. In 1860, the famous freighting company of Russell, Majors, and Waddell (who had since joined the firm) established the Pony Express to deliver the mail from St. Joseph, Missouri, to California. William Russell ordered the establishment of 190 pony express stations across the West, situated between 10 and 15 miles apart.

Young men, many just teenagers, were hired to ride the mail as quickly as possible from one station to the next. The mail was placed in specially designed leather pouches, called mochilas, which fitted over the rider's saddle. At each stop, the mochila was transferred to a fresh horse and rider, and the mail was carried to the next station. In all, the Express hired 200 horsemen and maintained 500 horses at all times.

While the Pony Express was a private business, it received support from the federal government, which provided a subsidy of over $1 million annually. Nevertheless, mail delivery by the Pony Express was costly, with an initial postage rate of $10 an ounce for a letter. (The amount was later dropped to $2 an ounce.) In all, the Pony Express delivered 34,000 pieces of mail.

The service was a logistical success, as the young riders were able to deliver mail on a regular 13-day schedule from St. Joseph to San Francisco. But the company proved a financial disaster, failing to produce a profit and leaving its investors with a $200,000 loss. During its 18 months of service, the Pony Express witnessed the erection of a telegraph line which followed the Express route. Two days after the telegraph line across the West was completed, on October 22, 1861, the Pony Express was shut down, ending an exciting chapter in frontier history.

Review and Write

1. What factors caused the Pony Express to fail in making a profit?

2. As more Americans moved into the western regions of the continental United States, the need for more efficient transportation systems increased. What types of groups needed better transportation in the west?

Test V

Part I.

Matching. *Match the answers shown below with the statements given above. Place the letters of the correct answers in the spaces below.*

1. Region which comprised the modern-day states of Washington, Idaho, and Oregon
2. American fur entrepreneur who established a trading post on the Columbia River in 1811
3. Native American name for Oregon Trail
4. American president who had campaigned for annexation of Oregon as American territory
5. Name given smaller wagon model used frequently on the Oregon and other western trails
6. Author of pioneer guide commonly used on the Oregon Trail, published in 1831
7. Rest stop on the Oregon Trail which marked one-third of the distance to Oregon
8. Opening in the Rocky Mountains allowing Oregon Trail pioneers to cross Continental Divide
9. Site along Oregon Trail pioneers hoped to reach by July 4 each emigrating season
10. Site in Oregon which was common goal for many pioneers on the Oregon Trail
11. Dreaded disease which sometimes struck western wagon trains on the Oregon Trail
12. Presbyterian missionary who established mission near Walla Walla, Washington

A. Marcus Whitman	B. Independence Rock	C. Jackson Kelley	D. Big Medicine Path
E. John Jacob Astor	F. prairie schooner	G. South Pass	H. cholera
I. Oregon Country	J. James K. Polk	K. Fort Laramie	L. Willamette Valley

1. ____ 2. ____ 3. ____ 4. ____ 5. ____ 6. ____ 7. ____ 8. ____ 9. ____ 10. ____ 11. ____ 12. _____

Part II.

Matching. *Match the answers shown below with the statements given above. Place the letters of the correct answers in the spaces below.*

1. Founder of the Church of Jesus Christ of Latter-Day Saints
2. Name used by Mormons to refer to all others who were not members of their sect
3. Illinois settlement for Mormons where they flourished and built a temple in early 1840s
4. Angel who delivered the content of the Book of Mormon to founder of the Saints
5. River claimed by Mexico as the southwestern border of Texas after Texas revolution
6. Treaty ending Mexican-American War
7. Transcendental writer who refused to pay his taxes as protest of Mexican War
8. Site of Mexican defeat in February, 1847 at hands of U.S. commander Zachary Taylor
9. American general who landed at Veracruz and marched troops to Mexico City
10. President of the U.S. during the Mexican-American War
11. Swiss ranch owner on whose property gold was discovered in California in 1848
12. U.S. Army officer and explorer who helped foment the Bear Flag Revolt

A. Nauvoo	B. James K. Polk	C. Winfield Scott	D. John C. Fremont
E. Gentiles	F. Neuces	G. Buena Vista	H. Johann Sutter
I. Joseph Smith	J. Moroni	K. Henry Thoreau	L. Guadalupe Hidalgo

1. ____ 2. ____ 3. ____ 4. ____ 5. ____ 6. ____ 7. ____ 8. ____ 9. ____ 10. ____ 11. ____ 12. _____

The Western Stagecoach

Perhaps no other form of transportation used across the West has become more symbolic of the spirit of the frontier than the stagecoach. These great, four-wheeled "buses" of the West provided passenger service, mail delivery, and light freight transport throughout much of the 19th century. In fact, stagecoaches mirrored the western movement, providing transportation along the East coast, through the Trans-Appalachian region, as well as the Trans-Mississippi West.

The history of the stagecoach dates back to 18th-century Europe. The first lengthy stagecoach line in America was established in 1785, running from New York City to Albany, the state capital. But these early stages were egg-shaped, lighter and smaller than English coaches. They did not use springs to make the ride less jarring, but rested the coach body on leather straps. But these early American models were, perhaps, too small. Passengers could not completely stand up in them and the coaches were not designed to carry baggage on top.

In 1813, a New England wagonmaker changed the future of stagecoaches forever. Lewis Downing lived in Concord, New Hampshire. He and his assistant, Stephen Abbot, designed a new type of stagecoach, lighter, yet with stronger wheels. Abbot also changed the shape of the coach so that baggage could be stored on top. This redesigned stagecoach was soon known as the Concord coach. Concord coaches were soon in use around the world, from England to Australia. Over the years, the team of Downing and Abbot changed their design several times, improving it each time.

It was a model of craftsmanship and design. The Concord coach was more comfortable than earlier coaches. Passengers entered the coach through either of two doors, each featuring a glass window that could open and shut, depending on the weather. There were also other windows, and leather curtains which kept out the cold weather. The sides of the coach curved out, but the earlier egg-shape design was gone. The top of the coach was surrounded by a brass railing to keep baggage

from sliding off, and a platform at the rear was designed to hold additional cargo and luggage. This platform was covered with a black oiled leather canopy which formed a weatherproof boot.

The coach body was built out of hardwoods such as white ash and white oak. The side panels were steamed into shape and dried on templates to ensure a tight fit when the pieces were constructed together. Concords were painted with several coats of red, blue, yellow, or green paint. It was then rubbed down and coated with two coats of spar varnish, which waterproofed the coach and gave it a brilliant sheen. Each door might feature a picture painted by an artist. The name of the company buying the coach was painted in gold above the doors. The coach's steps were painted black and the brakes and gears painted yellow.

Inside the coach, passengers could occupy any of three seats, allowing nine to ride in relative comfort. People sitting in the front row sat with their backs to the driver, while the other two seats faced the horses. A tenth rider could sit outside alongside the stagecoach driver.

The Abbot and Downing light stagecoach weighed approximately 2,500 pounds and sold for $1200, a significant price in the 19th century. Throughout the 1800s, Abbot and Downing sold hundreds of stagecoaches to western companies, including the Butterfield Line and Wells, Fargo, & Company. Few stages were built after 1900, but Abbot and Downing remained in business another 20 years, building mostly truck bodies and fire engines.

Indian Resettlement

By the end of President James K. Polk's single term in office, extraordinary developments had taken place across the Trans-Mississippi West. As early as Polk's first year in the White House, 5,000 had already traveled the entire length of the Oregon Trail, and thousands more were lining up to join them. In 1846, the United States and Great Britain agreed on the dividing of the Oregon Country. Following the Mexican War, the lands from California to Texas were joined to the Union. Over the following decades, Congress granted territorial status to Utah, New Mexico, Washington, Dakota, Colorado, Nevada, Arizona, Idaho, Montana, and Wyoming.

Through the 1850s, American eyes remained fixed on the West and its varied frontiers. California and Oregon became states on both ends of the decade—California in 1850 and Oregon in 1859. The American imagination for moving west seemed to know no bounds when, in 1867, the U.S. purchased Alaska from the Russians. With the movement of people into the West, the federal government went, as well, providing forts for protection on western trails, providing mail delivery service, and building frontier roads, just as previous generations of American leaders had provided its pioneers in the Trans-Appalachian West.

Among the responsibilities of the U.S. government was the increasing administration and control of the western Indian tribes. This was not a new responsibility by the 1850s, but the process was constantly evolving. After the establishment of an Indian Territory in what is today Oklahoma, Kansas, and a portion of eastern Nebraska in the 1830s, a process of forced migration relocated many tribes in the Trans-Mississippi West. Most of the tribes who moved into the region under government stewardship in the 1840s and '50s had originally lived east of the Mississippi River.

The southern portion of the Indian Territory was home to the Native Americans of the Southeast—Cherokees, Chickasaws, Choctaws, Creeks, and Seminoles. In the northern portion, tribes from the original Northwest were settled—Delaware, Wyandot, Shawnees, Sauks, Foxes, Potawatomis, Miamis, Kickapoos, Ottawas, and Peorias.

But the removal of these tribes did not solve the Anglo-American Indian problem. It merely postponed it. In addition, there were many tribes of the Great Plains and the Rocky Mountain region who were becoming restless in their own right, anxious at the increasing numbers of non-Indians moving across and settling on their land. These tribes included the Cheyennes, Arapahoes, Comanches, Kiowas, Blackfeet, Crows, Utes, Shoshonis, Nez Perce, and Salish peoples. In the Southwest, today's Arizona and New Mexico, lived the Pueblos, Hopis, Acomas, Zunis, Pimas, Papagos, Apache bands, and the Navajos. While the policy of Indian removal in the East had resulted in the moving of tribes into the Trans-Mississippi West, such a policy toward these additional tribes was out of the question, for where could they be moved where non-Indians did not already live?

Then, to make matters worse, in 1854, the U.S. Congress established the western territories of Kansas and Nebraska for non-Indian settlement. With this move, the tribes which had been resettled in that northern half of the Indian Territory, again lost their lands to government policy. New treaties were arranged and tribes from the Sauk to the Delaware, the Miamis to the Omahas, and the Foxes to the Piankashaws agreed to accept smaller reservations as home.

82

Indian Warfare on the Plains

In 1865, by the end of the Civil War, there were approximately 360,000 Native Americans living in the Trans-Mississippi West, with many still occupying the same lands on the Great Plains they had occupied for generations. The policy of relocation of Eastern tribes to the West had caused increased stress and pressure on Native Americans who were competing for natural resources. Native Americans became uncertain as to which way to turn. As a result, a trend toward armed conflict developed.

Even a generation before the Civil War, American officials had determined the best policy toward Indians was one through which Indians accepted life on limited, specified reservation lands under government supervision and protection. Through a series of treaties made with the U.S. government, Native Americans in the West were restricted in their movements and where they could call home. In 1867, the Medicine Lodge Treaty assigned the Comanches, Kiowa, Apaches, Cheyennes, and Arapahoes to reservations.

Other Plains Indians attempted to remain unrestricted on the open lands of the Great Plains, especially north of the Indian Territory, by then the Nebraska Territory. But free-roaming bands of Lakota (Sioux), Pawnees, and Crow met resistance from Anglo-American miners, settlers, and military personnel stationed across the West.

In addition, the presence of increasing numbers of non-Indians was threatening the Native American way of life on the Great Plains. For example, through mass slaughter of the Plains bison (buffalo) by professional buffalo hunters, the great herds which had, in earlier generations, blackened the Plains with their numbers, were being reduced.

The ease with which non-Indian hunters eliminated buffalo was particularly unsettling. Armed with a new .50 caliber Sharps rifle, a professional buffalo hunter could pick off unsuspecting buffalo at a distance of 600 feet. Dozens might be downed daily by one hunter. Some hunters bragged that they had killed

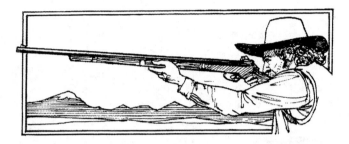

thousands in their short-lived careers. Ironically, these buffalo were generally killed only for their hides and their tongue, a delicacy served in eastern restaurants. (Buffalo bones were later collected and ground up into fertilizer.) With ever decreasing numbers of available buffalo for use by the Great Plains tribes, these Native Americans were losing control of their culture, their primary food source, as well as their lands. Pressed with few options, some Indians on the Plains chose to fight rather than watch their way of life die.

Just as previous Indian leaders in the East— Pontiac, Tecumseh, Black Hawk and others— had rallied Native Americans to take a stand against non-Indian encroachment on their lands, so a new generation of Indian leaders gave the same call. Early action broke out in Colorado in 1864, when the territorial governor John Evans terminated all treaties with tribes in eastern Colorado after several Cheyenne raids resulted in several deaths, rapes, and mutilations of white residents. Evans then encouraged white residents, called the Colorado volunteers, to attack Cheyenne villages and encampments.

Cheyenne chief, Black Kettle, responded by gathering his people (approximately 800) at Fort Lyon for safety. After settling along Sand Creek, a group of Colorado militia, many of them drunk, led by Colonel John Chivington, attacked the encampment of men, women, and children. During the massacre, 105 Cheyenne women and children, as well as 28 men (most of the men were out hunting during the attack) were killed. In response, Cheyenne, Sioux, and Arapahoes retaliated by attacking white settlements.

Clashes on the Great Plains

The series of conflicts which followed the infamous Sand Creek Massacre primarily involved the Lakota people, or the Sioux. From 1865-67, the Great Sioux War brought warriors under the leadership of Lakota chief, Red Cloud, into armed conflict with the U.S Army. The fighting was centered along the Bozeman Trail in the Big Horn Mountains region near the border between Montana and Wyoming. The Lakota were concerned about the presence of army forts in the region and the violation of their territory by non-Indian miners.

Red Cloud claimed that the government-built Bozeman Trail from Fort Laramie, Wyoming to the gold camps of Montana destroyed the region's best buffalo-hunting grounds. Thousands of warriors followed Red Cloud, a counter of 80 coups, wiping out a detachment of fewer than 100 soldiers near Fort Phil Kearney on December 21, 1866. Eventually, the government abandoned the road, leaving the region completely. Red Cloud and his warriors then burned the evacuated forts.

The Treaty of Fort Laramie was signed in 1868, granting large tracts of reservation land to the Lakota and the Northern Cheyennes in the Dakota, Wyoming, and Montana Territories. Even after peace was restored in the West, the conflicts were not over. Following Red Cloud's victories, the Indian policy of the U.S. Army took a harsh turn. Some western generals, including the great Civil War commander, General William Tecumseh Sherman, insisted that the only viable policy toward Indians was one of extermination.

By 1874, a new series of conflicts emerged. Chief Red Cloud had taken up residence on a reservation, but another generation of Indian leaders stood ready, including the Teton Sioux Chief Crazy Horse and a Hunkpapa Sioux named Sitting Bull. Despite the establishment of Indian lands in the Dakota Territory, which had closed the region to any and all white encroachment, rumors circulated that gold had been discovered in the Black Hills, a portion of the Dakotas which the Lakota people

held as sacred. When U.S. Army Colonel George Armstrong Custer, a hero of the Civil War, marched an expedition into the Black Hills to prove the rumors false, the opposite occurred.

The Dakota Territory was soon overrun with eager gold seekers, and the Lakota people and their leaders found themselves pushed off their lands once again. In fact, some Lakota had never accepted reservation status, including Sitting Bull, who was technically at war with the United States from 1869 until 1876. Crazy Horse joined with Sitting Bull in 1875 to stand against white gold miners and to remain independent from the U.S. government.

Among the Army officers who fought the Lakota and their allies was Colonel Custer, who marched his men onto sacred Lakota lands to erect a fort. Commanding the Seventh U.S. Cavalry, in pursuit of the Lakota and Cheyenne led by Sitting Bull, Custer arrived at the junction of the Big Horn and Little Horn Rivers, west of the Rosebud Mountains in Montana on the evening of June 24, 1876. His scouts informed him of the presence of a small contingent of warriors.

Without proper information and foolheartedly dividing his men, Custer fell into a trap as his cavalrymen attacked the Indians on June 25. With a force of only 265 men, Custer found himself facing between 2,000 and 4,000 hostile Native American warriors. His entire force was wiped out in a battle which the soldiers called the Little Bighorn (after a nearby river), and which Indians referred to as the battle of the Greasy Grass (their name for the same river).

Review and Write

1. What Native American concerns caused them to decide to fight the U.S. Army?

2. The Great Sioux War came to an end with the signing of the Treaty of Fort Laramie. Why didn't this treaty end the conflicts between whites and Native Americans in the west?

Subjugating the Plains Indians

The Custer Massacre, commonly referred to as "Custer's Last Stand," was a short-lived victory for the Native Americans of the Great Plains. After that encounter, the U.S. Army fought across the West with a vengeance, tracking down dissident Indian factions with an urgent swiftness. By 1877, the Lakota campaign was completed. Crazy Horse was dead, killed at an American post. Lakota leaders surrendered their rights to the Black Hills, which they called Paba Sapa, and the members of the various bands were reestablished on government-administered lands.

Other Native Americans continued fighting, including the Apaches in the Southwest. Even after their great chief, Cochise, had surrendered to the Army in 1872, agreeing to take his people to a reservation, other Apaches fought on under Cochise's successor, Geronimo, who continued a guerrilla war against white miners and the U.S. military.

The Red River War of 1874–75 brought Apache bands in alliance with Kiowas and Comanches. The war was an extremely bloody one, but the Army brought most of the combatants under control by 1875. However, Geronimo continued fighting, hiding in the hills of his homeland, until 1886, when he finally surrendered.

The desire for more and more land in the West even led the U.S. government to go to war with tribal nations which had traditionally been at peace with the United States. When gold was discovered on the traditional lands of a friendly people known as the Nez Perce in 1860, government agents demanded the Native Americans surrender 90 percent of their lands, a total of 6 million acres.

Some Nez Perce leaders agreed to the demands, but others refused, including Chief Tukekas. He and many of his people had converted to Christianity. In protest against the land encroachment of whites, Tukekas abandoned his Christian faith, threw away his Bible and returned to his native religion. His son, Chief Joseph, led a band of his people against the U.S. government when agents attempted to force the Nez Perce to move to a reservation.

Through a series of encounters with U.S. troops, Chief Joseph's people fought bravely and generally outmaneuvered every attempt to recapture them. In 1877, Chief Joseph attempted to take his 750 followers, including women and children, north toward Canada, to escape the hands of the Army. Through a 1,400-mile march, fleeing the Army at every turn through the Bitterroot Mountains of Idaho, across Wyoming and Montana, Chief Joseph and his people were finally captured in northern Montana. In less than four months, Joseph had fought 2,000 U.S. troops and 18 Indian auxiliary detachments through two major battles and 18 skirmishes. But, in the end, his people were placed on a reservation in Oklahoma.

By 1880, nearly every Indian tribe in America had been subdued, removed from their traditional lands, and forced onto reservations. As early as 1871, the U.S. government had stopped recognizing the Indians as sovereign nations with legitimate land claims, thus ending the era of treaty making.

The new government policy became one of assimilation. This government approach to Indians was embodied in the Dawes Severalty Act, passed by Congress in 1887. Under this act, the reservation lands were broken up and distributed to individual Indians in allotments of 160 acres for each family head. This ended the era of communal ownership of Indian property. Such Indians were encouraged to farm, but few either wanted to or understood how. The days of the once powerful Native American tribes was over.

Review and Write

1. Why was the Dawes Severalty Act a poorly considered government decision?

2. Despite the victory of the Lakota and Cheyenne against General George Armstrong Custer and his 7th calvary, how did events turn against these Native Americans by 1877?

The Transcontinental Railroad

The movement and permanent settlement of the Trans-Mississippi West led to the destruction of the Native American way of life. One aspect of that movement was the extension of the railroad across the western plains, extending the iron rails to the California coast. The building of the first transcontinental rail line and the subsequent growth of western railroads is a story of endurance, political intrigue, technological advancement, and the permanent alteration of the American frontier.

A railroad across the continental United States—a transcontinental railroad—had been talked about in America since the 1840s, as a means of delivering freight, mail, and passengers to

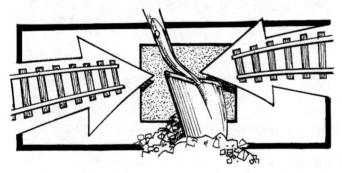

California and points between. But the building of such a line was delayed by political infighting in Congress over where the route should be built. With the issue of the spread of slavery into the western territories, northerners wanted to build a northern route, while southerners saw the need for a southern route, one which would encourage the development of slavery in the Southwest region.

As Congress debated during the 1850s, Eastern railroads moved further and further west. A rail line crossed Wisconsin to the Mississippi River by the mid-1850s. A direct line between Chicago and Iowa was opened with the building of the Rock Island Bridge over the river in 1856. The Hannibal & St. Joseph Railroad reached the banks of the Missouri River in 1859. In all, four or five railways were laying track across Iowa and Missouri by the end of the decade.

The outbreak of the Civil War ultimately decided

the issue. When the southern states seceded from the Union in 1860–61, northerners in control of Congress voted for a northern route, extending from Chicago to San Francisco. President Abraham Lincoln signed the Pacific Railway Act on July 1, 1862. Rail lines already ran from Chicago to Council Bluffs, Iowa, so the building actually began near Omaha, Nebraska.

Such a construction project would require more capital investment than any one company in America could raise, so it was determined that two companies would be needed to build the western line. The Central Pacific Railroad started in California and moved east, while the Union Pacific laid track across Nebraska and Wyoming, starting near Omaha. The two railroads were to meet somewhere in between. A standard rail width was established at 4 feet, 8.5 inches, so the tracks of both railroads would match when they met.

The railroads were granted major concessions for their commitment to build the first continental line. The federal government promised subsidies to the railroads for each mile of track constructed. The lines were paid $16,000 per mile of track laid across flat prairie land, while a mile of plateau or desert track paid $32,000. A mile of mountain track collected a subsidy of $48,000. In addition, each railroad received a right-of-way—the land adjacent to the tracks—of 400 feet. As an additional incentive, the railroads would receive 6,400 acres of land for every mile of track constructed, and that amount was doubled in 1864.

Groundbreaking for the new transcontinental railroad took place on December 2, 1863, when the Nebraska territorial governor, Alvin Saunders, unearthed a few shovels of frozen Nebraska topsoil during an outdoor ceremony. But a year and a half would pass before even the first rails were laid.

Review and Write

Why was the building of a transcontinental railroad delayed until 1864?

The American Frontier

Completing the Western Rails

Inexperience and a lack of available materials and labor slowed down the building of the transcontinental railroad before it even began. The first rails laid near Omaha were not put down until July 10, 1865. The construction crews were awkward and inefficient, taking eleven days to put down the first mile of track. Five months later, only 30 miles had been laid west of Omaha.

By early 1866, the Union Pacific Railroad employed a new, efficient engineer named Grenville Dodge, a general and veteran of the Civil War. Dodge reorganized the Union Pacific's construction efforts and sped up the process of laying track. When the tracks reached the 100th meridian, 240 miles up the Platte River from Omaha, the railroad's vice-president, Dr. Thomas C. Durant, held a great celebration, hosting such notables as future president Rutherford B. Hayes of Ohio. The festivities included a buffalo hunt, a mock Indian attack, and a controlled prairie fire.

At year's end, the Union Pacific workers had laid track as far west as North Platte, Nebraska, nearly 300 miles out of Omaha. Through the next year, that railroad had built as far west as Cheyenne, Wyoming, and by the end of 1868, the Union Pacific had built their line into Utah, not far from Ogden. Many of the workers on the Union Pacific were recent immigrants from both Germany and Ireland. Veterans of the Civil War and former slaves also worked on railroad construction.

The push and drive of construction for the Union Pacific Railroad was a pair of brothers, Jack and Dan Casement, who organized the day-to-day building efforts. The Casements put together construction trains complete with everything from dining cars to kitchen cars to blacksmith's shop to a telegraph office. They ordered sleeping cars capable of housing 100 men each. A herd of cattle was maintained to provide the men with fresh meat. They offered incentives to the hard working men, including a pound of tobacco for laying one mile of track in a day.

At the opposite end of the transcontinental

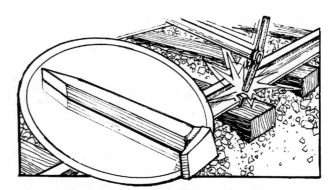

line, the Central Pacific workers struggled against great natural obstacles, including desert land and the rugged peaks of the Sierra Nevadas. Chinese immigrants provided much of the labor for the Central Pacific construction crews. Such workers often had experience with explosives which were used in blasting out tunnels from the granite of the Sierra Nevadas.

It took the Central Pacific workers nearly three years to cut their way through the mountains, but by 1868, crews built track quickly across the Nevada flats. While Union Pacific workers had occasional problems with local Native Americans who attacked and killed railroad men, the Central Pacific had few such incidents. Bosses on the Central Pacific sometimes handed out free tickets to local Indian chiefs.

After four years of construction, the two railroads finally met at a site north of Ogden, Utah, called Promontory Point. On May 10, 1869, the rail line was complete. The Union Pacific had constructed over 1000 miles of track while the Central Pacific had put down nearly 750 miles. A special celebration took place on the frontier with dignitaries in attendance from all over the United States, including the Governor of California, Leland Stanford. When the governor was granted the privilege of driving in the last spike, completing the line, he swung his steel hammer, missing the spike altogether.

But the lines were linked, bringing the country together through a symbolic ribbon of steel. Other transcontinental railroads followed. By 1890, four such lines crisscrossed the West, and by 1893, a fifth line was completed.

The Western Cattle Industry

While the Great Plains had been home for thousands of years to millions of buffalo, the 19th century witnessed the dramatic decline of these rugged, woolly animals. Native Americans hunted them in increasing numbers, at a rate faster than the animals could naturally multiply. By the early decades of the 1800s, some Plains tribes were killing six or seven buffalo per tribal member annually.

But the wholesale destruction of the plains bison took place at the hands of the professional buffalo hunter. Such men were so deadly efficient in their work that the millions of buffalo located across the Great Plains in 1800 had been reduced to perhaps fewer than 1,000 by 1890. With their dwindling numbers went the way of life for many Native Americans.

Yet as the numbers of bison were reduced in numbers, another animal took its place as a prominent animal of the Great Plains. At the close of the Civil War, an estimated 5 million head of longhorn cattle roamed the grasslands of southern Texas. These free-ranging cattle were descendants of Spanish cattle herds.

In the spring of 1866, an Illinois-born cattleman named Joseph G. McCoy (later in life, he worked as a treasury department narcotics agent) announced Abilene, Kansas, as the western terminus for shipping Texas cattle to eastern markets. The demand for beef during the Civil War to feed the enlisted men had created a shortage of cattle in the northern states. At the same time, due to immigration, the American population had risen by more than 20 percent, causing a greater demand. From Abilene, cattle could be shipped east on the Kansas Pacific Railroad to slaughterhouses in Kansas City, St. Louis, and Chicago.

McCoy hoped that enterprising cattle herders would drive Texas longhorn north to Abilene. In 1867, approximately 35,000 head reached McCoy's stockyards in Abilene. But the years immediately following saw even greater numbers of cattle for shipment east.

Once drivers realized the potential for profit, the cattle drives from Texas—typically called "The Long Drive"—became a source of quick riches. In 1868, for example, one cowman purchased 600 steers for an average of $9 a head, investing about $5,400. In Abilene, he sold his herd for $16,800, netting himself, after expenses, a $9000 profit, double his initial investment. By 1871, cowboys herded 190,000 head of cattle to Abilene. Other Kansas "cow towns" also received herds, such as Dodge City, which received 200,000 in 1882.

Cowboys utilized a number of significant trails for herding their cattle north to eastern markets. The oldest of the routes, the Shawnee Trail, swung northeast through the Indian Territory into southeast Kansas and Missouri. At its northern end, the trail split off, ending at either Kansas City, St. Louis, or Sedalia, Missouri. Another trail—the Goodnight-Loving—was named for two cattle men, Charles Goodnight and Oliver Loving. This route was established in 1866, and delivered cattle through western Texas, into New Mexico, across Colorado, where cattle might be shipped east on either the Atchison, Topeka, & Santa Fe Railroad or the Kansas Pacific, which had reached west to Denver. A third trail, the most famous of all, was the Chisholm Trail.

Named for a half-Indian trader named Jesse Chisholm, this route was formed by a combination of several Texas trails which joined at Red River Station on the northern Texas border. From there, the trail ran north across Indian Territory to the Cimarron River where it branched again, toward Dodge City, Abilene, and other Kansas cow towns and rail heads.

Review and Write

1. Although the bison had roamed the Great Plains region for thousands of years, by the early 1800s, their numbers were dwindling. Why?

2. How did the non-Indian, professional buffalo hunters of later decades speed up the process of killing off the Great Plains bison herds?

The Myth of the Cowboy

The enduring image to emerge from the days of the Long Drives, which lasted approximately 15 seasons, was, of course, the cowboy. The subject of countless motion picture and television westerns, the cowboy remains the figure most synonymous with the Trans-Mississippi West; a rugged individual who carried a handgun on his hip and always fought for the underdog.

But the real image of the cowboy is one based less in romance and more in the practical work-a-day nature of driving cattle and managing livestock. The typical cowboy took his cues from his Spanish predecessors, the vaqueros, who worked Spanish and Mexican ranches in the American Southwest in the 18th and early 19th centuries. The vaqueros developed the typical cowboy costume, including a wide-brimmed hat to protect the face from the sun, leather chaps to protect legs from prairie cactus, leather vest, bandanna around the neck to protect from sunburn and dust, and a rope always close at hand.

The cowboys who worked the Long Drive were paid low wages, usually $30 per month, which was paid at the end of the drive. This often meant the cowboy, newly arrived in a cattle town with saloons and gambling houses, often spent his money recklessly, with little to show for months of grueling, dusty, dangerous work. Due to the difficult working conditions on the trail, cowboys often developed serious back problems or came up lame in one leg. They spent much of their time dirty, hair unkempt, and were often missing some teeth, hardly

the romantic picture seen in the Westerns.

Cowboys were an ethnically diverse group. One out of three was Indian, Mexican, or black. Many of the black cowboys had been slaves prior to the Civil War and had worked cattle on southern plantations. In some cases, their fathers might have been cattle handlers in Africa prior to being brought to America as a slave.

A common and enduring myth concerning cowboys was their tendency to use handguns, causing the deaths of anyone who got in their way. This was rarely the case. For example, Dodge City witnessed only 5 murders during its ten seasons as a rail head for cattle drives. In fact, Dodge City saw more murders before its cattle days, when, during one, Dodge City was the site of 15 murders. Taken together, the cowtowns of Abilene, Ellsworth, Wichita, Caldwell, and Dodge City saw fewer than two murders during each cattle-trading season.

The years of the cattle drives were short-lived. By the 1880s, the era was over, replaced by the establishment of permanent ranches which dotted the Western landscapes of Colorado, Nebraska, Wyoming, Montana, and New Mexico. Such ranches maintained regular herds, bred them, and refrained from selling them until the price of beef was high. New breeds were introduced, including beefier Herefords and Angus imported from England.

By the 1880s, the cattle business was a corporate entity of the West, with large ranch owners—often called "cattle barons"— operating their enterprises as joint-stock companies, funded by eastern capital, similar to the corporate mines of the same era.

Following a pair of harsh winters on the Great Plains in 1884–85 and 1886–87, the cattle industry experienced a decline, as herds suffered in numbers. At the same time, an increasing number of western farmers and sheep ranchers were occupying the West, challenging the control previously wielded by cattlemen whose ranches might include thousands of acres of open range.

The Homestead Act

During the 1840s and 1850s, as frontier farmers moved further and further west, they typically avoided moving beyond the Great Plains. The Plains were considered too barren for farming— too dry for raising crops, grains, or even supporting domesticated livestock. By 1860, the furthest extension of western settlements generally followed a line stretching from St. Paul, Minnesota, to Fort Worth, Texas, then swung south toward the Rio Grande. Much of the Plains region between Texas and Canada, and between St. Joseph, Missouri, and Denver remained unoccupied by farming communities.

Before the end of the 1860s, this region would experience extensive migration. One source of the change was a mounting propaganda campaign launched by several regional newspapers, transportation officials, and visitors to the Midwestern prairies. One such writer, after visiting the Red River Valley of northern Dakota in 1869, penned: "The soil is of the richest sort and easily cultivated for there is neither stone nor stump to bother the plow." Already, would-be western farmers were provided a major incentive through a significant piece of legislation passed by Congress in 1862.

Known as the Homestead Act, a farmer could make application for 160 acres of government land at no cost, other than a five- or ten-dollar filing fee. The pioneer farmer was to build a dwelling on the property and live on his land for five years. At the end of those years, the government granted him full title to the property. Any settler wanting to take possession and ownership earlier, after only six months, could pay $1.25 an acre and receive immediate title. A later act, passed in 1871, and called the Timber Culture Act, granted an additional 160 acres free to any settler who planted 40 acres of trees on the property. (The number of acres was later reduced to ten.)

The Homestead Act opened up millions of acres of western land and thousands of eastern farmers took advantage of the opportunity. The initial homestead was filed on January 1, 1863, near Beatrice, Nebraska. But the real homesteading drive occurred in the late 1860s, and early 1870s. In 1871 alone, there were 20,000 homestead claims filed and 2.5 million acres of public land occupied on the Minnesota-Dakota border and across the Nebraska-Kansas frontier. Between 1871–72, Kansas saw 9,000 homestead claims. Then, in the mid-1880s, a great spate of homestead filings occurred, as a second generation of Plains farmers attempted to establish roots on the prairies. Dakota Territory experienced 22,000 filings in 1883, and Kansas saw 43,000 homesteads filed between 1885–87.

Homesteading, however, proved difficult on the Great Plains. When Congress enacted the law, few legislators gave any thought to farmers moving further west than the 100th meridian, into western Kansas, Nebraska, and the Dakotas. East of the line, a typical growing season received adequate rainfall to support cultivation. But when farmers moved west of the line, into the arid West, success was more difficult. In that region, 160 acres was not enough land, since survival often hinged on raising cattle, which required more land as well as crops and grains.

Additional problems plagued those who attempted farming on the Plains. Without available trees, the farm families often lived in a house made of sod. Also, homestead farms were often remote, with no close neighbors, which fostered loneliness. And such farms might often be far from viable transportation systems needed to deliver farm produce to markets of any size.

Review and Write

1. Why were homesteads established west of the 100th meridian riskier than those established to the east?

2. What was the migration pattern across the Great Plains during the 1840s and 1850s? What caused a serious and significant change in the pattern by the 1860s?

Immigration to the Great Plains

With the advancement of the railroads across the West; with the realization that the Great Plains could be reasonably farmed; and with government incentives to put down roots across the Trans-Mississippi West, the vast open expanse of the Great Plains and Rocky Mountain frontier was soon populated by thousands, even millions of non-Indians. By the last decade of the 1800s, the hand-writing was on the wall for Native Americans who found themselves simply outnumbered at a ratio of approximately 40 to 1.

Such rapid growth would not have been possible without the development of the railroads, which offered families convenient transportation west, and a delivery system for getting their farm produce to eastern markets. As railroads encouraged settlement, they published tracts, posters, and other printed information, boasting the advantages of Western farm life. Railroads even sent agents to Europe to convince dissatisfied Europeans to immigrate to America.

Between 1870 and 1900, they came by the trainload, a total of two million European immigrants arriving and settling across the Great Plains. Some regions of western territories and states saw entire pockets of Europeans establish themselves in close-knit communities. Some counties in Minnesota were home to large groups of Swedes, while other communities became home to groups of Finns. Across the Dakotas, Scandinavians made up 30 percent of the population, with Norwegians representing the largest group. As early as 1870, one out of every four residents were foreign born, having drawn large numbers of Germans, Swedes, Danes, and Czechs.

To the south of Nebraska, the percentage of newly arrived European immigrants during the final decades of the 19th century was lower, with some exceptions. By 1900, Germans constituted one-third of the white population of the state of Texas.

While life could be lonely, remote, and difficult on the Great Plains, many of the ethnically based communities thrived and prospered. Some Nebraskans joked about how "living in Nebraska is a lot like being hanged; the initial shock is a bit abrupt, but once you hang there for awhile you sort of get used to it."

The immigrants' lands were typically square claims, homesteads of 160 acres. As a weapon against loneliness, farm families sometimes built their houses and barns on a shared corner of adjacent properties so they would have a few close neighbors.

Western frontier communities soon dotted the landscape of the Great Plains. Such towns as Grand Island, Nebraska, nestled along the banks of the Platte River, Coffeyville, Kansas, Sioux City, Iowa, and Fargo, North Dakota, established in the midst of thriving farming districts, became the centers of commerce, social interaction, and local politics.

Settlement in such towns occurred as rapidly as the outlying lands were populated. Although the Civil War slowed the process of western town development, there was a significant increase in frontier town growth over the decades to follow. By 1890, towns could be found all along the central grasslands at intervals of approximately six to ten miles, a short enough distance to allow a buggy ride from one to the other and back home again, in the same day.

Common western town elements included a newspaper, a hotel, a city saloon, a blacksmith shop, a general store, a school, a church, and a bank. In addition, towns set aside land for the development of cemeteries.

Review and Write

1. What European national groups were making their way to the Great Plains between the 1870s and the turn of the century? In what part of the Great Plains did they settle?

2. What simple transportation fact sometimes determined how closely western towns might be located to one another across the Great Plains?

The Bounteous Plains

The final three decades of the 19th century witnessed great strides in the development of frontier farming and settlement. Through active solicitation by railroads, and the availability of cheap land, as well as encouragement from state and territorial governments, farmers took up residence in eastern Kansas and Nebraska between 1865 and 1875. By the latter date, farmers were moving further west, out onto the high plains. As the cattle drives came to an end in the early 1880s, more and more farmers moved into regions where cattle had previously dominated. When bumper crops were produced during 1883 and 1884, a great influx of western homesteaders took out land claims—2,000 in the spring of 1885 in Nebraska alone.

From 1880 through 1890, the number of farms in the United States rose by some 550 percent. In some cases, these farms were more than the usual single-family operations. In the region of the Red River valley of northeastern Dakota Territory, large-scale farms were established by the Northern Pacific Railroad. Known as Bonanza Farms, these experimental, corporate-owned agricultural operations included thousands of acres, used the latest mechanized equipment and employed hundreds of hired hands. Such farms produced

thousands of bushels of wheat per season.

Despite these efforts to turn farming into big business, most farms remained limited operations. A typical western farmer might start his homestead by planting a few acres in grain, such as oats, rye, or barley. In the Dakota Territory, wheat might be planted, while in Nebraska, corn crops were more common. In addition, the small farmer grew a variety of vegetables for his family's consumption and for surplus sale. He might have a few head of cattle or hogs and perhaps some poultry. Such farms were often self-sustaining and might reap limited profits for the farmer and his family. Cash was scarce on western farms, and a farming family might not see an annual income of more than $100 to $200. Over time, with more acreage under the plow, greater profits were often the result.

With the invention of better machinery, farmers across America found themselves more and more productive during the final decades of the 1800s. Such labor-saving devices as the John Deere plow, the McCormick reaper, plus bailers, binders, cream separators, and other machines forever changed the equation linking hand labor and productivity. For example, in 1890, the U.S. commissioner of labor estimated that, prior to the wire binder in 1875, the average western farmer could not expect to harvest more than eight acres of wheat without outside help. With the application of that single technology, a farmer in 1890 could harvest 135 acres of wheat. As a result, between 1880 and 1900, the size of the average farm in the seven states producing the most grain increased from 65 acres to more than 100 acres.

The story of the success of western farming is found in the numbers. In 1869, Kansas, Nebraska, and the Dakotas produced fewer than 5 million bushels of wheat. By 1900, the amount produced was more than 175 million. The number of cattle in these same states during these same years increased from 500,000 head to 13 million.

In addition, the populations of such Great Plains states had grown considerably. By 1890, the Dakotas, Nebraska, Kansas, and Oklahoma Territory were home to over 3 million non-Indian people, with 87 percent living in rural areas. Through 1889 and 1890, six new western states were added to the Union—North and South Dakota, Montana, Wyoming, Idaho, and Washington—signaling an end to the frontier.

──The Making of the Frontier Myth──

By the early 1890s, the signs were everywhere. The frontier movement was winding down, the hectic days of westward expansion were being tamed, and the lands of the Great Plains and the Far West were not only largely occupied, but they were also generally settled.

What scenes had been commonplace across the Trans-Mississippi West even a generation earlier were becoming visions of the past. The great buffalo trails had been turned into railroad lines,

and Native American villages transformed into reservations. Sod houses were giving way to substantial, middle-class farm houses, sturdy and strong. Rollicking frontier mining and cattle towns were nearly a thing of the past, having been replaced by brick streets, brick storefronts, and rock-solid citizens who voted for schools and strong law enforcement, and who built churches which competed for the town's faithful.

Without question, the land had been transformed and would continue to feel the impact of occupations looking ahead to the 20th century. Lands which had never witnessed Indian villages larger than a few thousand inhabitants were already supporting mid-sized cities of tens of thousands. Such western cities and even their smaller, rural counterparts swelled with civic pride—their residents boasting about the grandeur of their streets, their sandstone courthouse, the academic strength of their thriving town college, or the high entertainment taking place at the town opera house.

So much of the rough and tumble nature of the frontier had vanished before the end of the 19th century. Yet the myth-making of the West was already underway. As early as the 1860s, the first written "westerns" were sold as "dime novels," some

selling as many as 50,000 copies. One of the earliest, Edward Zane Carroll Judson's *Buffalo Bill, the King of the Border Men* (1869) was the first of many such examples of popular fiction about the West and its exciting frontier image.

Buffalo Bill, himself the subject of western myth-making, in time became one of the most significant myth-makers. Born in a log cabin in Iowa in 1846, William Frederick Cody served as a rider for the Pony Express, army scout, and buffalo hunter. One of his earliest jobs was as an express boy for the freighting firm of Majors & Russell, delivering messages by mule near Ft. Leavenworth, Kansas.

As a boy of 14, he rode for the Pony Express. Four years later, he served in the 7th Kansas Volunteer Cavalry during the Civil War. The next year, he and his friend, Wild Bill Hickok, served as army scouts. He earned his nickname, "Buffalo Bill," during the late 1860s, when he hunted for the Kansas Pacific Railway, providing meat for rail crews. The subject of dime novels and even stage plays by the late 1860s and early '70s, helped Buffalo Bill become famous.

But his real claim to fame as a myth-maker of the West came in 1882, when he staged a 4th of July celebration called "Old Glory Blow Out" in North Platte, Nebraska. The show included 1,000 cowboys with Cody demonstrating how he had killed buffalo in his earlier years. The next year, he opened the first of his "Wild West" shows in Omaha.

It was the beginning of a new era for Buffalo Bill and for the American West. From 1883 through 1916, Buffalo Bill starred in his Wild West shows, which toured 1,000 cities in 12 countries to a total audience of 50,000 awe-struck fans. The show included live action involving scores of performers enacting scenes of buffalo hunts, mock stagecoach robberies, and Indian battles. One of its most popular performers was the sharpshooter Annie Oakley. Sitting Bull himself was part of the show for a brief period. Buffalo Bill's Wild West shows helped to solidify the excitement of the frontier image for Americans for generations.

The Closing of the Frontier

By 1890, America was beginning to witness the end of a phenomena—one which had served as the centerpiece of America's early development and expansion across the vast North American continent. For some, the existence of the frontier and its stages of pioneer movement marked the calendar of American history, serving as a pulse regulating the nation's growth and the development of a uniquely American character.

One of the first to note the value of the frontier experience in American history was a young historian, Frederick Jackson Turner. Turner, a university professor in 1893, delivered a paper which he presented at a gathering of fellow historians during a world's fair called the Columbian Exposition (designed to celebrate the 400th anniversary of the European discovery of America by Columbus, although a year late).

Turner's paper was titled, "The Significance of the American Frontier." His main argument would come to be known as the "frontier hypothesis." It was Turner's contention that "the existence of an area of free land, its continuous recession, and the advance of American settlement Westward" explained the development of the United States geographically, physically, politically, socially, and psychologically. As Americans moved further west with each passing generation, the frontier was reborn. In Turner's words, each move west meant "a return to primitive conditions on a continually advancing frontier line." Turner's point: Each new frontier allowed Americans to again redefine themselves.

Turner saw a repeated pattern, then, to America's frontier experience. It was each of America's frontiers that served as "the meeting point between savagery and civilization." The young historian was clear about the stage of the pattern. First, the wilderness experience caused the pioneer to abandon his "civilized" appearance and take on the appearance of a frontiersman, as he put it, "the hunting shirt and the moccasin," reducing him to a primitive state similar to the Native American. But,

slowly, certainly, the frontier experience allowed the pioneer to transform his or her world, allowing for the transplanting of civilization and civilized institutions, such as law, government, church, school, as well as economic and trade systems. But each new generation of pioneers created a new civilization different from the previous one—one adapted from a new environment. Turner's claim was that with each new "civilization," the American became less European and more uniquely, distinctly American. Thus, the frontier experience resulted in "the formation of a composite nationality."

Turner's concept of the closing of the West was partially confirmed when, following the 1890 census, the superintendent of the census declared that there was no longer a frontier line in America. And while Turner's frontier thesis has remained an enduring theory, helping to explain the nature of Americans, it has proven inadequate at some turns. His contention that each new frontier devolved its inhabitants into primitive savagery is probably overstated. Turner's claim that each pioneer movement was forced, by its primitive surroundings, to abandon nearly all aspects of civilization is probably exaggerated as well. More often, pioneers carried civilization along with them as they moved.

But, without question, the American frontier experience was one which included both the more noble elements of the American character, as well as the darker side of our national identity. It remains behind us now, a memory growing dimmer with the passage of each new generation.

Review and Write

1. From your reading, do you think Turner's thesis concerning the frontier is valid?

2. What new reality concerning the American frontier was being recognized by the 1890s?

3. Who was Frederick Jackson Turner and what was the point of his famous "frontier thesis"?

Part I.

Matching. *Match the answers shown below with the statements given above. Place the letters of the correct answers in the spaces below.*

1. One of the designers of the Concord-style stagecoach; worked with associate Stephen Abbot
2. This 1867 treaty assigned the Comanches, Kiowa, Apaches, Cheyennes to reservations
3. Type of .50-caliber rifle used by professional buffalo hunters
4. Territorial governor who terminated all treaties with tribes in eastern Colorado in 1864
5. Colorado militia colonel who attacked encampment of Black Kettle's people at Sand Creek
6. Western trail in Montana and Wyoming which was focus of 1865–67 Great Sioux War
7. Lakota chief who led his people in Great Sioux War
8. U.S. Army colonel who led his men to disaster in the battle of the Greasy Grass in 1876
9. Nez Perce leader who fought a defensive war with U.S. Army in 1877
10. Act of Congress which broke up Indian lands and distributed 160 acres to family heads
11. Railroad company which began construction of transcontinental line in California
12. Site where the transcontinental line was completed and dedicated in May, 1869

A. Medicine Lodge B. John Chivington C. George Custer D. Central Pacific
E. Sharps F. Red Cloud G. Chief Joseph H. Promontory Point
I. Lewis Downing J. John Evans K. Bozeman L. Dawes Severalty Act

1. ____ 2. ____ 3. ____ 4. ____ 5. ____ 6. ____ 7. ____ 8. ____ 9. ____ 10. ____ 11. ____ 12. ____

Part II.

Matching. *Match the answers shown below with the statements given above. Place the letters of the correct answers in the spaces below.*

1. Illinois-born cattleman who established Abilene, Kansas, as western terminus for cattle markets
2. Process of herding cattle from Texas to Kansas cow towns during 1860-1870s
3. Name of 1866 cattle trail which delivered cattle through Texas into New Mexico to Colorado
4. Half-Indian trader who established cattle trail from Red River Station to Kansas towns
5. Spanish and Mexican predecessor to the American cowboy
6. Beefier cattle breed imported from England to western cattle ranches
7. U.S. government act which allowed a family to claim 160 acres of free, public land
8. U.S. government act which granted 160 acres to settlers who planted 40 acres of trees
9. Type of corporate farm established in the Dakota Territory by the Northern Pacific Railroad
10. University professor who developed his "frontier thesis" in 1893
11. Nebraska site of the first land claim filed under Homestead Act
12. Inventor of popularly-used mechanical reaper

A. Goodnight-Loving B. vaquero C. bonanza D. Timber Culture Act
E. Homestead F. Long Drive G. Hereford H. McCormick
I. Joseph McCoy J. Jesse Chisholm K. F.J. Turner L. Beatrice

1. ____ 2. ____ 3. ____ 4. ____ 5. ____ 6. ____ 7. ____ 8. ____ 9. ____ 10. ____ 11. ____ 12. ____

The United States 1783-1802

CANADA

MAINE
(joined to Mass)

Grand Portage ●   *Lake Superior*

Fort
Michilimackinac

Montpelier

Oswegatchie
Ft. Haldimand

Portland

Lake
Huron

Green
Bay

NEW YORK

Ft. Ontario
Oswego

Concord

Boston   MASSACHUSETTS

Lake Ontario

Albany

Fort Niagara

Providence

Lake Michigan

INDIANA TERRITORY

NORTHWEST TERRITORY

Detroit
Fort
Miamis

Lake Erie

Hartford

RHODE ISLAND
CONNECTICUT

Mississippi River

NORTHWEST TERRITORY 1800

Allegheny R.

New York
Trenton

NEW JERSEY

NORTHWEST TERRITORY 1787

Pittsburgh

PENNSYLVANIA

Philadelphia
Wilmington

Illinois River

Fort Recovery

Miami R.

Baltimore

DELAWARE

Wabash River

Cincinnati

Ohio River

Marietta

Washington
D.C.

MARYLAND

Vincennes

Cahokia
Kaskaskia

KENTUCKY
(admitted 1792)

TERRITORY SOUTH OF THE RIVER OHIO

VIRGINIA

Richmond

James River

Roanoke River

LOUISIANA

SPANISH

Cumberland River

Raleigh

NORTH CAROLINA

Nashville
TENNESSEE
(admitted 1796)

Fort San
Fernando
(Spanish)

Tennessee River

Columbia

SOUTH
CAROLINA

A t l a n t i c
O c e a n

GEORGIA

Chattahoochee River

Altamaha River

Savannah

Mississippi River

Northern Spanish Claim Until 1795

0   500 Miles

0   500 KM

Fort Nogales
(Spanish)
Natchez
Fort Adams

MISSISSIPPI
TERRITORY 1798

SPANISH   FLORIDA

The Northwest Territory, formed in 1787, was divided in 1800 as more settlers moved into the area. The western part became known as the Indiana Territory, while the eastern part continued to be called the Northwest Territory.

G u l f
o f
M e x i c o

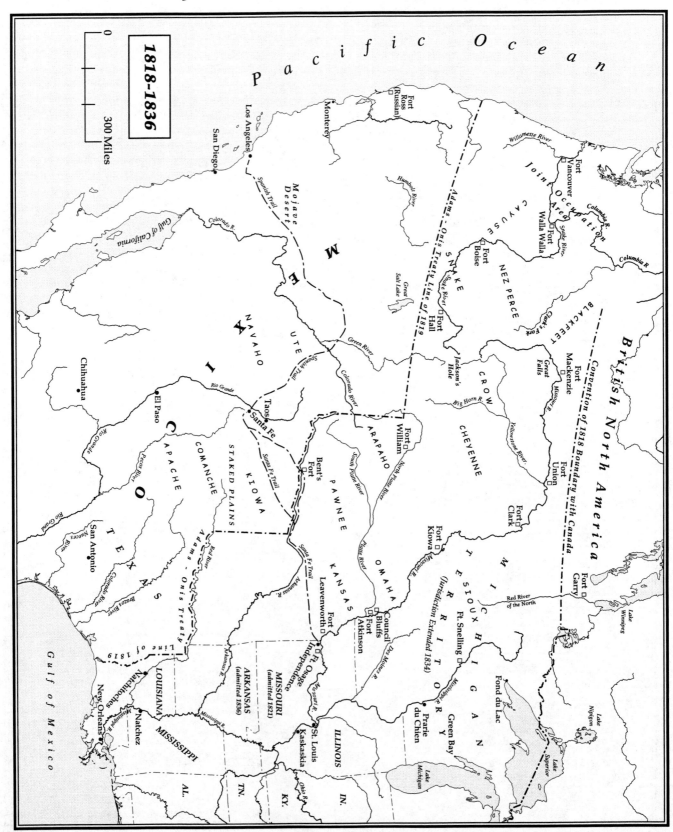

— Boundary Treaties & Western Advance —

1818-1836

0

300 Miles

Pacific Ocean

Fort Ross (Russian)

Monterey

Los Angeles

San Diego

Spanish Trail

Mojave Desert

Colorado R.

Humboldt River

Willamette River

Fort Vancouver

Columbia R.

Fort Walla Walla

Snake River

Fort Boise

Adams-Onis Treaty Line of 1819

Convention of 1818 Boundary with Canada

Joint Occupation Area

CAYUSE

NEZ PERCE

Clark's Fork

BLACKFEET

British North America

M E X I C O

N A V A H O

U T E

Green River

Great Salt Lake

Fort Hall

Jackson's Hole

CROW

Great Falls

Fort Mackenzie

Missouri R.

Big Horn R.

Yellowstone River

CHEYENNE

Columbia R.

Chihuahua

Rio Grande

El Paso

Taos
Santa Fe

Spanish Trail

Colorado River

ARAPAHO

Fort William

South Platte River

North Platte River

Fort Union

Fort Clark

Missouri R.

Red River of the North

Fort Garry

Lake Winnipeg

Rio Grande

Pecos River

APACHE

COMANCHE

Santa Fe Trail

Bent's Fort

Adams-Onis Treaty

STAKED PLAINS

KIOWA

PAWNEE

Platte River

OMAHA

Missouri R.

S I O U X   T E R R I T O R Y
(Jurisdiction Extended 1834)

Ft. Snelling

M I C H I G A N   T E R R I T O R Y

Fond du Lac

Lake Nipigon

Lake Superior

San Antonio

Nueces River

Colorado River

Brazos River

T E X A S

Red River

Adams-Onis Treaty Line of 1819

Fort Kiowa

KANSAS

Fort Leavenworth

Fort Atkinson

Council Bluffs

Des Moines R.

Red River of the North

Green Bay

Prairie du Chien

Lake Michigan

Gulf of California

Gulf of Mexico

New Orleans

Natchitoches

LOUISIANA

Natchez

MISSISSIPPI

Mississippi R.

Arkansas R.

ARKANSAS (admitted 1836)

MISSOURI (admitted 1821)

Ft. Osage

Independence

St. Louis

Kaskaskia

ILLINOIS

Missouri R.

Ohio R.

IN.

AL.

TN.

KY.

Westward Advance 1849-1860

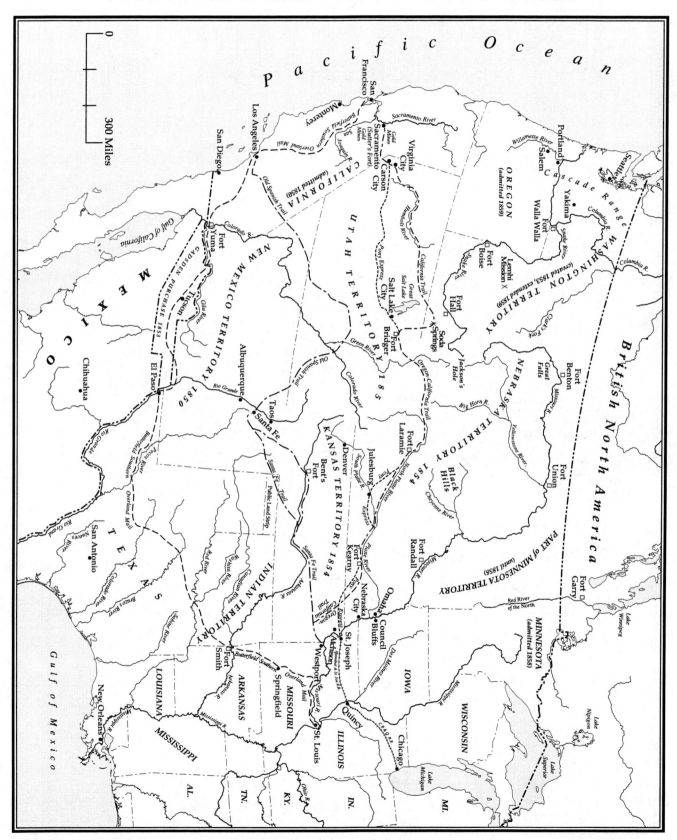

The Trans-Mississippi 1861-1865

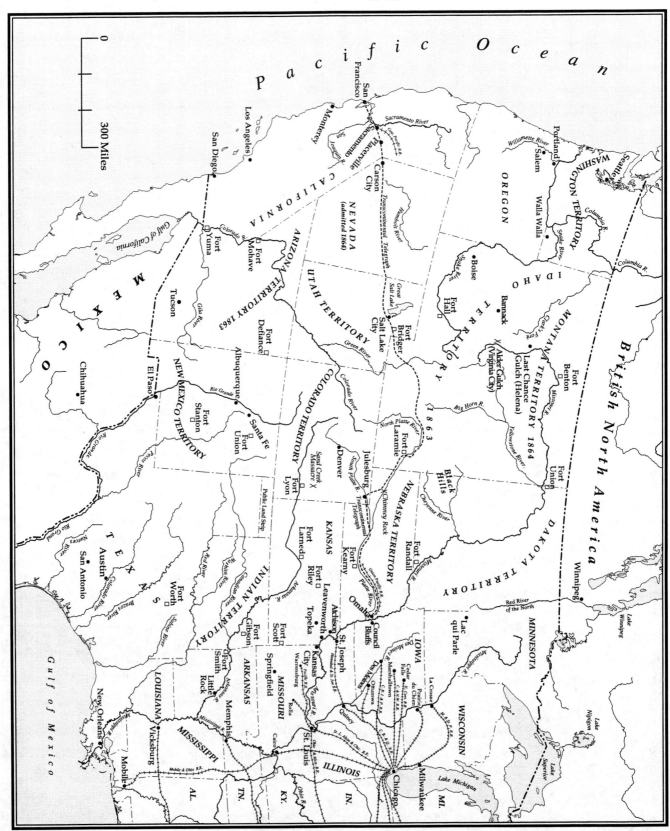

Answer Key

Page 2

When the term "the West" is used in connection with "the frontier," it is not only a direction, it is a region. And just as with the frontier, where "the West" was depended on where people were in time. As people moved west (meaning the direction, not the place), they established new settlements, each attached to a new wilderness place and the process of taming, the new "frontier" began all over again.

Page 3

The Trans-Appalachian region spans the land west of the Appalachian Mountains and beyond, to the lands lying just west of the Mississippi River. The time frame for this frontier movement spanned from 1750 to 1850 approximately. The Western Frontier, or Trans-Mississippi West, covered the years between 1850 and 1890 and was centered on the settlement of people across the Great Plains, west of the Mississippi River, throughout the Rocky Mountain region and the Pacific Coast.

Page 4

1. Most Indian trails were paths often no wider than 12 to 18 inches across. Warriors followed these paths single file, creating deep ruts sometimes a foot deep. Such trails typically followed the best routes between destinations, cutting around river bends, avoiding hill tops, and opening up to meadows thick with wildlife.

2. The Iroquois Trail: Ran from the Hudson River west, flanking the Mohawk River to Lake Erie, across modern-day New York. The Kittanning Path: Ran from Eastern Pennsylvania across the Appalachians through Kittanning Gorge. Beyond the mountains, the Kittanning reached the Allegheny River, which became the headwaters of the Ohio River. Warriors' Path: Ran from North Carolina to Ohio. One branch of this trail extended as far west as modern-day St. Louis.

Page 6

1. The first phase of economic growth in the Piedmont was focused on the fur trade and the establishment of trading posts along the Fall Line. The second phase was the development of the cattle industry, with Virginia 'cowboys' raising steers and horses. The third phase was the settling of the region by pioneer farmers, especially Germans.

2. The Piedmont is a plateau lying directly east of the Appalachian Mountains.

Page 9

1. The British lured Indian support for their cause, promising them they would take into consideration "the grievances complained of by the Indians, with respect to the lands which have been fraudulently taken from them." The British promised to establish a fixed border between English settlements on the frontier and the hunting grounds of the Native Americans.

2. General Amherst, now military governor of the region, banned the old policy of giving presents as peace tokens to the Indian chiefs and tribes of the frontier. He banned all trade with Native Americans involving guns and ammunition.

Page 10

1. The Proclamation of 1763 declared the lands which Pontiac was fighting for off limits to Anglo-American migration and settlement.

2. Amherst distributed blankets infected with the smallpox virus to the Native Americans.

Page 13

1. Boone met Finley when the two men were involved in Braddock's march into eastern Pennsylvania in the summer of 1755. Finley told Boone of the hunter's paradise to be found in Kentucky, which Finley had visited. In 1768, Finley and Boone were reunited when Finley arrived at Boone's selling wares as a peddler. Boone recognized his old friend and through Finley's renewed stories, Boone was inspired to trek into Kentucky.

2. When he was only ten years old, young Boone learned the ways of the woods. Local Indians taught him how to survive in the wild, how to track animals, plus other frontier skills. His father gave him his first rifle at age 12. In his teen years, Boone hunted to provide food for his family. He traded the animal pelts for supplies.

Page 15

1. Families moved into the Powell and Holston Valleys east of the Cumberland Gap. Others occupied lands on the French Broad river. These settlements were known as the Watauga Settlements.

2. The area was ideal for farming, including rich land and an advantageous climate. Access to Tennessee was easier by road by the late 1770s. A third incentive was cheap land.

Page 16: Test I

Part I.
1. F   2. K   3. G   4. B   5. I   6. E   7. H   8. C   9. A   10. J   11. D   12. L

Part II.
1. D   2. E   3. J   4. A   5. H   6. I   7. G   8. B   9. K   10. F   11. L   12. C

Page 19

The Conestoga was one of the most durable wagons ever built and a pioneer who had one could travel just about anywhere. This wagon, built with German craftsmanship, was capable of hauling several tons of cargo.

Page 22

1. Trees had to be cut and shaped. They were dragged to the cabin site behind horses. The pioneer used his froe to split some of the better logs. The outer walls were constructed and a roof put into place. The cracks between the logs had to be filled with mud, sticks, stones, or other materials.

2. Pioneers would construct an open-sided "lean-to" made of tree branches and bark. Otherwise, the settlers lived in their wagon or even slept outdoors.

Page 24

The Second Continental Congress realized the importance of making alliances with various Indian tribes on the frontier against the British. The British understood the same things. Indians allied themselves on both sides, but most tribes sided with the British.

Page 25

1. Clark intended to gather a force of frontiersmen, and march them down the Ohio River to capture British outposts in the Illinois Country.

2. They had to fight Indians along the way and sometimes make alliances. Clark and his men made a legendary march through the winter, suffering through icy waters and freezing temperatures.

Page 26

1. Despite the Proclamation of 1763, western migration had never ceased.

2. By 1785, the non-Indian population of Kentucky had mushroomed to more than 30,000. By the end of the decade, another 45,000 had joined them. In Tennessee, 36,000 immigrants had established their frontier homes.

Page 29

1. Jay's Treaty brought an agreement from the British to abandon the last of their forts in the Old Northwest which they had never surrendered under the Treaty of Paris (1783). Jay's Treaty was a great diplomatic victory for the young U.S., which eliminated any significant presence by the British on American soil. Pinckney's Treaty reopened the Spanish-controlled Mississippi River to American trade traffic once again. This was great news for many of those Americans living in the Trans-Appalachian region. They needed to rely on access to the Mississippi and the Spanish port of New Orleans for shipping their western produce to market.

2. Wayne forced Native Americans to sign the Treaty of Greenville, which ceded the southern half of Ohio to the United States, giving the American government a new footing in the frontier region. John Jay negotiated a treaty with Great Britain calling for the elimination of any significant presence by the British on American soil. Thomas Pinckney negotiated with the Spanish over the southern boundary of the U.S. and the reopening of the Spanish-controlled Mississippi River to American trade traffic once again.

Page 30

1. The Alaskan natives destroyed a fleet of Russian ships. After four years of fighting, the Aleuts were finally destroyed.

2. In the 1740s, Peter the Great had sent a Danish sea captain, Vitus Bering, on an expedition to Alaska. His voyage revealed the abundance of furs, sparking others to follow in his footsteps. By the 1750s the Russians had established an extensive trading empire in Alaska. By 1784, Russian merchant Gregory Shelikhov established the first permanent Russian settlement in Alaska. By the turn of the century, the Russian-American Company had established a series of fur trading bases from Alaska to San Francisco Bay.

Page 32: Test II

Part I.
1. D   2. E   3. A   4. J   5. F   6. B   7. K   8. G   9. C   10. L   11. H   12. I

Part II.
1. I   2. H   3. A   4. J   5. F   6. B   7. K   8. G   9. C   10. L   11. E   12. D

Page 33

1. Cincinnati developed as a significant western meatpacking center. Other industries developed including soap, shoes, boots, and candles.

2. In its early years, Cincinnati was little more than a fort intended to protect pioneers living along the Ohio and Miami Rivers. Indian attacks were common and violence involving various tribes caused the region to be know as "the Slaughterhouse." After the 1794 battle of Fallen Timbers, Cincinnati was on its way. The town first developed as a popular site of departure for frontier families headed down the Ohio River.

Page 37

1. The engineering required for the Erie Canal was highly sophisticated. The canal was to be 40 feet wide, four feet deep, and 364 miles in length. Three hundred bridges would also need to be built so people on either side of the canal could cross over it. The canal required the construction of 83 locks, special water chambers designed to raise and lower boats passing along the full length of the canal. In addition, the work would involve removing thousands of tree stumps and blasting rock out of the canal's path.

2. During the early decades of the 19th century, the federal government built roads such as the National Road. Also, states funded the construction of toll roads, canals, and railroads to facilitate the movement into their regions. In the 1820s alone, states spent $26 million on "internal improvements."

Page 38

1. The arrival of the steamboat on the frontier changed the history of the Trans-Mississippi West. New Orleans became the most important port in America. In 1801, the value of the goods passing through New Orleans was about $4 million. Through the 1840s, New Orleans handled twice the amount of the goods that were shipped through the port of New York City.

2. By 1830, this inexpensive transportation system brought 50,000 people to the West. New towns

sprang up and older communities received a shot in the arm from the economics created by the waterway.

Page 41

The objectives were to extend the American fur trade to the tribes throughout the region, to advance geographical knowledge of the continent, and to establish friendly relations with the Indians.

Page 42

1. The expedition collected new plant and animal specimens. They also collected scientific information including soil samples, weather information, and geological knowledge.

2. Most of the men were in their 20s, eager to participate and nearly all of them were unmarried.

Page 44

The members of the Corps of Discovery experienced Indian encounters, buffalo hunts, high mountain crossings on horseback, the collecting of natural specimens, grizzly bear attacks, and outstanding scenery.

Page 47

1. The Spanish were concerned that Pike was on a spying mission for the United States, assessing the potential for the region to become an American acquisition.

2. Pike continued his journey south, toward Spanish territory.

Page 48: Test III

Part I.
1. E   2. I   3. A   4. J   5. F   6. B   7. K   8. G   9. C   10. L   11. D   12. H

Part II.
1. I   2. E   3. A   4. G   5. F   6. B   7. K   8. J   9. C   10. L   11. H   12. D

Page 51

1. By defeating the Creeks, Andrew Jackson was able to extract a new series of land cessions by Native Americans to the American government. Under the Treaty of Fort Jackson, the Creeks surrendered 23 million acres of traditional lands, half of those claimed by the tribe's leaders.

2. Mohawk and Geness Turnpike: Across New York to Lake Erie; Lancaster Turnpike: Ran from Philadelphia to Pittsburgh; National Road: Began in Baltimore and extended west; Wilderness Road and Saluda-Cumberland Gap: Used by southerners; Federal Road: Ran south around the southern end of the Appalachians.

Page 52

1. The Cherokee had become viable farmers, taking on many aspects of white culture and practice. Indian villages might represent white towns and settlements, complete with houses, farms, orchards, blacksmith shops, and other indicators of Indian assimilation. The Cherokee raised large acreage of corn, kept herds of cattle and hogs, and grew cotton with black slaves providing the work force. They used modern tools, rifles, spinning wheels, and looms, even built gristmills for grinding their grain into flour. They wore white men's clothing, developed a written language, printed their own newspaper, and even wrote their own constitution. Many of them had converted to Christianity.

2. The Gulf Plains includes the territory extending along the Gulf of Mexico from Florida to the lower banks of the Rio Grande River, extending north in a triangle shape to the juncture of the Ohio and Mississippi Rivers. The land features prairies with rich soils, where timber was available in abundance. The climate is relatively mild and highly suitable to the cultivation of cotton.

Page 54

For seven years, Osceola led his people, hiding women and children and encouraging his fighters to hit and run against a stronger enemy. Their resistance was a success, for a time.

Page 57

1. In 1821, the Mexican people successfully carried out a revolution against the Spanish. Once Mexico was firmly in Mexican hands, the trading town of Santa Fe was opened to American traders.

2. The Santa Fe Trail connected Missouri settlers, traders, and businessmen with their Mexican counterparts in the frontier town of Santa Fe. The colonial Spanish government feared the arrival of Americans and looked at each such arrival with suspicion.

Page 58

Between 1790 and 1840, the entire region from the Atlantic to the Mississippi River had been carved into states, except for Florida and Wisconsin. Some migration had also taken place out onto the Great Plains region.

Page 59

While the Louisiana Purchase did bring a vast territory of over 800,000 square miles under the jurisdiction of the U.S. government, it was a risk to move further west to places such as Texas, Arizona, California, or Utah—places claimed and occupied by European powers such as Great Britain and Spain.

Page 60

1. The land grants doled out by Mexican authorities were generous. Many other Americans migrated into Tejas, so there were neighbors from the same place. In addition, an economic depression in the U.S., called the Panic of 1819, dispossessed some Americans and caused severe economic problems for many.

2. In 1821, the Mexicans overthrew the Spanish. Following that revolution, the Mexicans became intent on settling the vast open regions of their northern provinces. Thus, they opened up the region of Tejas to immigrants, including those from the United States.

Page 62

1. Austin originally campaigned for moderation, but when it became clear that reconciliation with Mexico was not possible, he gave support to the revolution, writing to a friend: " War is our only recourse. We must defend our rights, ourselves, and our country, by force of arms."

2. Americans were, through earlier frontier experiences, an unruly and aggressive group. When authorities attempted to reestablish their authority in Texas, the Texans interpreted such steps as a challenge, leading them to take up arms against the Mexicans.

Page 65

1. Behind the denial of Texas statehood was the burning question concerning slavery in the United States. Many northerners, including Congressman John Quincy Adams, could not abide by the admission of a 14th slave state into the Union, and blocked Texas admission. Adams was the leader of the northern opposition.

2. 1) They could remain an independent republic, 2) They could attempt to create an even larger, independent state by campaigning south against Mexico itself, 3) They could attach themselves to England or France by alliance, and 4) They could apply for U.S. statehood.

3. John Quincy Adams was opposed to Texas statehood because it would bring another slave state into the Union.

Page 66: Test IV

Part I.
1. G   2. E   3. A   4. J   5. F   6. B   7. K   8. I   9. C   10. L   11. H   12. D

Part II.
1. I   2. H   3. A   4. J   5. G   6. B   7. K   8. F   9. C   10. L   11. E   12. D

Page 69

The pioneers hunted animals on the trail to provide meat for their consumption. Leftover milk was placed in a watertight pail and suspended from the back of the wagon. After a day's jostling, it became butter. They picked up firewood and dried buffalo chips for fuel.

Page 70

1. Fort Laramie was one-third of the entire distance along the trail. At this fort, the pioneers could buy supplies, get their wagons repaired, and talk with others about the trail ahead.

2. Some pioneers continued southwest toward California (the California Trail), while others stayed on the Oregon Trail which continued on in a northwest direction toward Idaho and Oregon.

Page 72

Deaths might occur from wagon accidents, gunshot wounds, drowning, buffalo stampedes, poisoning by alkali water, suffering heart attacks and strokes from overexertion, appendicitis, and disease.

Page 73

1. The sect was founded in 1827 by a New Yorker named Joseph Smith, who claimed to have been visited by an angel, named Moroni, son of the prophet Mormon.

2. Smith had been killed by a mob and Young emerged form the ranks of the Mormons to become the president of the sect.

Page 74

1. The controversy was over the annexation of Texas as an American state. When the United States claimed Texas to include the land north of the Rio Grande, the Mexicans were furious.

2. Polk ordered General Zachary Taylor to have his troops take up positions along the banks of the Rio Grande in defiance of the Mexicans.

Page 77

1. San Francisco became a boom town filled with thousands of miners, prospectors, entrepreneurs, and card sharks. Mining camps experienced high rates of inflation. The influx of miners and others caused the number of Californians to swell to 100,000, making statehood possible by 1850.

2. Forty-Niners was the nickname given to the people who rushed to California in 1849 to seek a fortune in gold. Four out of every five were Americans. In addition, about thirteen percent were from Mexico and Latin America. Another seven percent came from Europe. Thousands of Chinese also came to California at the height of the gold rush.

3. Life was expensive in the camps as high inflation drove prices through the roof. Life in the camps could also be dangerous, disappointing, and even monotonous.

Page 79

1. Mail delivery by the Pony Express was costly, with an initial postage rate of $10 an ounce for a letter. The line itself was expensive to operate, requiring the building and maintenance of nearly 200 Pony Express stations across the West. In addition, the Express hired 200 horsemen and maintained 500 horses at all times.

2. Pioneers living in Oregon and California, those living in mining towns, and those working in corporate mines.

Page 80: Test V

Part I.
1. I 2. E 3. D 4. J 5. F 6. C 7. K 8. G 9. B 10. L 11. H 12. A

Part II.
1. I 2. E 3. A 4. J 5. F 6. L 7. K 8. G 9. C 10. B 11. H 12. D

Page 84

1. The Native Americans were concerned about the presence of army forts in the region and the violation of their territory by non-Indian miners.

2. Even after peace was restored in the West, the conflicts were not over. After Red Cloud's victories, the Indian policy of the U.S. Army took a harsh turn. Some western generals insisted that the only viable policy toward Indians was one of extermination. By 1874, a new series of conflicts emerged.

Page 85

1. It ended the era of communal ownership of Indian property. Such Indians were encouraged to farm, but few either wanted to or understood how. The days of the once powerful Native American tribes was over.

2. After the encounter, the U.S. Army fought across the West with a vengeance, tracking down dissident Indian factions with an urgent swiftness. Crazy Horse was dead by 1877, and the members of the various Lakota bands were reestablished on government-administered lands.

Page 86

The building of such a line was delayed by political infighting in Congress over where the route should be built. With the issue of the spread of slavery into the western territories, northerners wanted to build a northern route, while southerners saw the need for a southern route, one which would encourage the development of slavery in the Southwest region.

Page 88

1. Native Americans hunted them in increasing numbers, at a rate faster than the animals could naturally multiply. By the early decades of the 1800s, some Plains tribes were killing six or seven buffalo per tribal member annually.

2. Such men were so deadly efficient in their work that the millions of buffalo located across the Great Plains in 1800 had been reduced to perhaps fewer then 1000 by 1890.

Page 90

1. East of the 100th meridian, a typical growing season received adequate rainfall to support cultivation. But when farmers moved west of the line, into the arid West, success was more difficult. In that region, 160 acres was not enough land, since survival often hinged on raising cattle, as well as crops and

grains, which required more land.

2. During the 1840s and 1850s, pioneer farmers avoided moving beyond the Great Plains. The Plains were considered too barren for farming and too dry for raising crops, grains, or even supporting live stock. A change in the pattern came about with the passage of the Homestead Act in 1862.

Page 91

1. Minnesota became home to the Swedes and Finns. The Scandinavians settled in the Dakotas, as well as the Norwegians. In Texas, the Germans found a home.

2. Towns could be found all along the central grasslands at intervals of approximately six to ten miles, a short enough distance to allow a buggy ride from one to the other and back home again, all in the same day.

Page 94:

1. *Answers will vary.* Much of the thesis still holds water today and can still be argued effectively. The material on this page raises some questions about the validity of the thesis by mentioning that his contention that each new frontier devolved its inhabitants into primitive savagery is probably overstated. In addition, students may note that Turner's claim that each pioneer movement was forced, by its primitive surroundings, to abandon nearly all aspects of civilization is probably overstated, as well.

2. That the frontier was closing and coming to an end.

3. Turner was a university professor during the 1890s. His frontier thesis was that, as Americans moved West, each new frontier allowed Americans to again redefine themselves. Each new movement west had produced "a return to primitive conditions on a continually advancing frontier line."

Page 95: Text VI

Part I.
1. I   2. A   3. E   4. J   5. B   6. K   7. F   8. C   9. G   10. L   11. D   12. H

Part II.
1. I   2. F   3. A   4. J   5. B   6. G   7. E   8. D   9. C   10. K   11. L   12. H

Bibliography

Ambrose, Stephen E. *Nothing Like It in the World: The Men Who Built the Transcontinental Railroad, 1863-1869* (New York: Simon & Schuster, 2000).

—*Undaunted Courage: Meriwether Lewis, Thomas Jefferson and the Opening of the American West* (New York: Simon & Schuster, 1997).

Andrist, Ralph K. *The Long Death: The Last Days of the Plains Indians* (New York: Macmillan Publishing Company, 1964).

Bartlett, Richard A. *The New Country: A Social History of the American Frontier, 1776-1890* (New York: Oxford University Press, 1974).

Beebe, Lucius and Charles Clegg. *The American West: The Pictorial Epic of a Continent* (New York: Bonanza Books, 1955).

Bonvillain, Nancy. *Native Nations: Cultures and Histories of Native North America* (Upper Saddle River, New Jersey: Prentice-Hall, 2001).

Botkin, *Daniel. Passage of Discovery: The American Rivers Guide to the Missouri River of Lewis and Clark* (New York: Berkeley Publishing Group, 1999).

Brady, Cyrus *Townsend. Indian Fights and Fighters* (Lincoln: University of Nebraska Press, 1971).

Bringhurst, Newell G. *Brigham Young and the Expanding American Frontier* (Boston: Little, Brown, 1986).

Brown, Dee. *Bury My Heart at Wounded Knee: An Indian History of the American West* (New York: Henry Holt & Company, 1970).

Brown, Mark H. and W.R. Felton. *The Frontier Years: L.A. Huffman, Photographer of the Plains* (New York: Bramhall House, 1955).

Carnes, Mark C. and John A. Garraty. *Mapping America's Past: A Historical Atlas* (New York: Henry Holt and Company, 1996).

Commager, Henry Steele. Ed. *The West* (New York: Promontory Press, 1976).

DeVoto, Bernard. *The Course of Empire* (Boston: Houghton-Mifflin, 1952).

Dick, Everett. *Tales of the Frontier: From Lewis and Clark to the Last Roundup* (Lincoln: University of Nebraska Press, 1963).

Edmunds, R. David. *Tecumseh and the Quest for Indian Leadership* (New York: HarperCollins, 1984).

Eide, Inguard Henry. Ed. American Odyssey: The Journey of Lewis and Clark. Chicago: Rand McNally, 1969.

Gibson, Arrell Morgan. *The American Indian: Prehistory to the Present* (Lexington, Mass.: D.C. Heath & Company, 1980).

Grant, Bruce. *Concise Encyclopedia of the American Indian* (New York: Wings Books, 1989).

Hafen, Leroy R. *Trappers of the Far West* (Lincoln: University of Nebraska Press, 1965).

Holloway, David. *Lewis & Clark and the Crossing of North America* (New York: Saturday Review Press, 1974).

Josephy, Alvin M. *The Indian Heritage of America* (Boston: Houghton-Mifflin, 1968).

Lavender, David. *The Great West* (New York: American Heritage, 1965).

Marks, Paula Mitchell. *Precious Dust: The American Gold Rush Era: 1848-1900* (New York: William Morrow and Company, 1994).

McNeese, Tim. *America's Early Canals* (New York: Macmillan Publishing Company, 1993).

—*America's First Railroads* (New York: Macmillan Publishing Company, 1993).

—*Conestogas and Stagecoaches* (New York: Macmillan Publishing Company, 1993).

—*Early River Travel* (New York: Macmillan Publishing Company, 1993).

—*From Trails to Turnpikes* (New York: Macmillan Publishing Company, 1993).

—*Illustrated Myths of Native America: The Northwest, Southeast, Great Lakes, and Great Plains* (London: Cassell Books, 1998).

—*Illustrated Myths of Native America: The Southwest, Western Range, Pacific Northwest, and California* (London: Cassell Books, 1999).

—*West by Steamboat* (New York: Macmillan Publishing Company, 1993).

—*Western Wagon Trains* (New York: Macmillan Publishing Company, 1993).

Merk, Frederick. *History of the Westward Movement* (New York: Alfred A. Knopf, 1978).

Mintz, Steven, Ed. *Native American Voices: A History and Anthology* (St. James, New York: Brandywine Press, 1995).

Perrigo, Lynn I. *The American Southwest: Its People and Cultures* (New York: Holt, Rinehart, and Winston, 1971).

Rohrbough, Malcolm. *The Trans-Appalachian Frontier: People, Societies, and Institutions, 1775-1850* (Belmont, California: Wadsworth Publishing Company, 1990).

Russell, Don. Ed. *Trails of the Iron Horse: An Informal History by the Western Writers of America* (Garden City, New Jersey: Doubleday & Company, Inc., 1975).

Schlissel, Lillian. *Women's Diaries of the Westward Journey* (New York: Schocken Books, 1982).

Tunis, Edwin. *Frontier Living: An Illustrated Guide to Pioneer Life in America, including Log Cabins, Furniture, Tools, Clothing, and More* (New York: Thomas Y. Crowell, 1961).

Utley, Robert M. *Frontier Regulars: The United States Army and the Indian, 1866-1891* (Lincoln: University of Nebraska Press, 1973).

— *Indian Wars* (New York: American Heritage, 1977).

Waldman, Carl. *Atlas of the North American Indian* (New York: Facts on File Publications, 1985).

Webb, Walter Prescott. *The Great Frontier* (Lincoln: University of Nebraska Press, 1951).

Wishart, David J. *The Fur Trade of the American West, 1807-1840* (Lincoln: University of Nebraska Press, 1979).

Wetmore, Helen *Cody. Buffalo Bill: Last of the Great Scouts* (1899) (Reprint: Stamford, Connecticut: Longmeadow Press, 1994).